Naked Goes My Heart

Rosalie,
God bless you,
You're special,
Pat Bavardo

Naked Goes My Heart

Patricia Bavardo and Sue Bosio

Northwest Publishing, Inc.
Salt Lake City, Utah

Naked Goes My Heart

For information address: Northwest Publishing, Inc.
6906 South 300 West, Salt Lake City, Utah 84047

JC 4.14.95 / JP

PRINTING HISTORY
First Printing 1995

ISBN: 1-56901-349-7

NPI books are published by Northwest Publishing, Incorporated,
6906 South 300 West, Salt Lake City, Utah 84047.
The name "NPI" and the "NPI" logo are trademarks belonging to
Northwest Publishing, Incorporated.

PRINTED IN THE UNITED STATES OF AMERICA.
10 9 8 7 6 5 4 3 2 1

This is biographical work.
Certain names have been changed to protect
the privacy of individuals herein.

Dedication

To and for you…all the girls and women who are living with emotional pain and are surviving. You're so special!

Pat Bavardo

This book is dedicated to women everywhere who've lived and loved the rollercoaster ride of life.

An enormous debt of thanks goes to my husband, John Bosio, who believed I could do it and watched the kids, made the meals, and did chauffeur duties while I wrote.

I'd also like to thank my children, Celeste and Alicia, for bringing such joy into my life every day.

Sue Bosio

In my opinion, life can sometimes be like
trying to eat a bowl of ice cream with a warm fork.
It can be done, but it sure as hell isn't easy.
Pat Bavardo

When life gives you lemons, do what I do—
make whiskey sours.
Sue Bosio

1

The noon sun blazed down on the old red brick railway station, baking the wooden platform and the people on it. Heated railroad tracks shimmied and danced in the searing heat as the cicadas sang in the trees. Usually by late September, the fall weather began to set in, turning the evenings cool and filling the days with a mellow, golden haze. But this summer of 1945, Freeport, Illinois was suffering through dreadful heat, with temperatures and humidity that kept most people inside near their window fans, or sitting beneath the shade of the elms in lawn chairs, with a frosty glass of iced tea in hand.

Despite the insufferable heat, today was a special day for four-year-old Meg O'Conner. Her daddy was coming home from the war. She stood beside her mother on the railway platform and fidgeted in her new dress and black patent leather shoes. It was the most beautiful dress she'd ever had, her favorite color blue, with little harlequins dancing across the skirt. Her mother, Irene, had bought the new clothes last week for Meg's fourth birthday, and for her to wear especially today.

"Meg, be careful of that dress and those shoes," Irene warned her harshly. "I paid good money for those clothes, and you know how careless you are. You have to stay clean for your father."

Meg glanced nervously at her feet and noticed that her shiny new shoes had a powdering of dust covering them. She squatted down and took one of Teddy's paws and wiped the dirt off her shoes until she could again see her reflection. Reaching up, she adjusted the bow in her hair, smoothed her bangs, and patted her bobbed hair just like she'd seen her mother do. She didn't know why her mother thought she had to be warned about her clothes. She would certainly take good care of them. New clothes for Meg were a rare treat. Usually she got hand-me-downs and cast-offs from the children of her mother's friends. Today she was alive with pride and excitement. She felt beautiful in her new finery, and her heart was filled with hope and happiness, anticipating meeting her daddy and having a real family, all of them together at last.

Little Meg had often studied the picture of her father on the living room table at home, wondering what he was like. Would he be nice? Would he be fun to be with? She would often whisper her deepest secrets to his picture. In the picture that Meg had studied so intently and touched so often, he had sandy-colored hair and looked tall and thin. Meg thought she looked a lot like him. He probably laughed real loud and hearty just like Grandpa O'Conner. He was smiling in the picture, as if he'd just heard a funny story, so Meg knew in her heart he'd be as nice as he looked. He just had to be.

Today he was coming home at last! James O'Conner had been gone since the spring of 1941. He was in the Army, 33rd Division, 124th Field Artillery, and had never met his little girl. He only knew her through the pictures Irene had sent to him, pictures now tattered and dog-eared.

Meg was an astonishingly beautiful little girl, with thick blonde hair and green eyes that flashed with the enjoyment of every day of life on this earth. She looked nothing like her mother, who was short and dark-haired, a little on the heavy side, from Pennsylvania Dutch and German stock. Irene's forbidding countenance manifested her stern and disapproving nature and outlook on life, her face like chiseled granite. Her straight dark hair reflected a no-nonsense style that somehow complemented her square face. Smiles were infrequent visitors to her face, and even her posture was ramrod stiff and full of reproach. At twenty-one, she reminded people of a strict schoolmarm.

Irene impatiently gazed down the tracks looking for the 12:15 Illinois Central train, which was taking a lifetime to arrive. The heat, the humidity, and her nerves were beginning to get to her. She unsnapped her purse, took her flowered hankie out and began dabbing at the perspiration on her brow and upper lip. She could feel rivulets of perspiration running from underneath her ample bosom. She snapped open her compact and studied her reflection, then carefully re-applied her carmine lipstick, deciding that would have to do.

From the station house, strains of Kate Smith crooning "Don't Fence Me In" hovered in the breathless, stifling air. It was a song Meg liked, one she could remember some of the words to, and in her excitement and suppressed joy, she danced around a little in time with the music. As she twirled, she noticed her mother looking in her compact, putting on her lipstick. She thought her mother looked pretty today, with her shiny new purse and high heels with the slim strap around her ankles. Meg tried walking on tiptoes so she would look taller and older than her four years. She wished she could wear lipstick, too. She stuck her pinky finger in her mouth and wet it with saliva, carefully applied the imaginary lipstick, and then started dancing again, spinning in joyous circles, her arms open wide to embrace the world.

Irene bent down and gripped her active daughter's arm firmly. "Meg, behave yourself. Stand still and act like a little lady. And don't talk so much, like you usually do." After her stern words, Irene reached around to adjust the seams in her stockings and straightened up to smooth the skirt of her dark green suit. Meg could tell her mother was nervous about seeing her daddy again, too. Meg, more than anyone, knew how very long four years could be.

The mournful sound of the train whistle pierced the hot, still air, announcing the train's impending arrival. The big black steam engine slowly chugged and chuffed around the bend, materializing magically in the wavering heat. In her excitement, Meg began jumping up and down and nearly lost her big blue hair bow. "Daddy's coming! I see the train, Mama! Daddy's coming!"

Suddenly she was frightened by the huge, loud train, with its billowing clouds of steam and screaming brakes, and she jumped instinctively away from the tracks and nearer to the old brick station house. There, from the safety of the benches, she could safely search for her daddy's face among the other travelers getting off the train.

When he stepped down from the passenger car, Meg recognized her daddy right away. He was tall, he did have sandy hair just like hers, and he did look just like his picture. He still wore his uniform, and Meg knew she'd never, ever seen anyone so handsome before.

"Daddy!!!" There was no stopping her. Meg's mind was racing as fast as her little feet as she ran down the platform and threw her arms around her daddy's legs. In her excitement, she dropped Teddy and had forgotten any and all fear of the big, black, puffing monster that now stood motionless on the tracks.

Jim hunkered down and scooped up his daughter, tossing her in the air and catching her in a bear hug on the way down. He hugged her so tightly it took her breath away, and a wave of love flooded her heart. Meg had known it would be like this. In her happiness, she hadn't even noticed the impatient frown on Irene's face.

With a crinkle in his hazel eyes, he laughed, "Well now, that's some greeting! How's my Meggy girl? At last I can hold you. You know, you're even prettier than your pictures, little Miss Sunshine. Oh, honey, it's so good to be home," he said, turning and looking around at his hometown.

He hugged her again and kissed her on top of her golden hair when he put her down. He began to pat around in the pockets of his jacket. "What's this lump in my pocket?" He made a big show of searching through his uniform jacket, which brought Meg suspenseful delight. Then he produced a small package and held it out to her. "Well, look here. It has your name on it, Sunshine. This just might be a birthday present for a special little girl, brought by her daddy all the way from the Philippines."

"A present for me?" Meg wasn't used to getting presents. She hesitantly took the crumpled package from his outstretched palm with trembling hands. "Can I open it now, Daddy?"

"You go right ahead, honey." He squatted on his heels at her level to watch. The joy in her face was like watching the sun come out from behind a cloud. Jim was acutely aware of all that he had missed in the past four years. "Damn war!"

She tore at the paper with the frenzy that only small children have when opening gifts. Inside was an intricately carved mahogany figurine of a little girl, gaily painted with brilliant colors. "Oh, Daddy!" With a squeal, she launched herself at him, hugging the new toy and her daddy possessively at the same time.

Irene stepped from the sidelines to join in the reunion,

a rare smile on her face. Touching his shoulder, she said, "Oh, Jim, it's so good to have you back home again! This has been the longest four years of my life."

He stood up and hugged his wife tightly, hungrily, and she returned the embrace, wiping at tears that were now streaming down her face. As Jim and Irene kissed, Meg watched with eyes open wide, a funny feeling in her tummy. She was glad to have her daddy home, but wasn't used to seeing her mother act in such a loving and emotional way. Meg was happy but just a little bit confused. She picked up her Teddy and hugged him tight, watching her parents with inquisitive eyes. Jim cleared his throat, trying to hold back the flood of emotion that had been bottled up for so long. He hugged Irene even tighter, not ever wanting to let her go again.

"Things haven't changed much here," her mother said as they relaxed from each other's embrace, a little embarrassed and ill at ease at the release of all these feelings. "Same old Freeport…never changes much. Come on, Jim, my mom and dad are waiting in their Buick to drive us over to your folks' house. Your mom is beside herself with excitement, waiting to see her Jimmy. I'm grateful that they've let Meg and me stay with them while you've been gone."

With concern in his voice, Jim asked about his mom, who had been bedridden for years with crippling arthritis. Irene brought him up to date on how his family was and continued, "My dad says you can have your job back as a shoe repairman at his shop. He knows you've had malaria and can't do strenuous work, so he wants to help. Oh, just listen to me ramble on. We have so much to catch up on, so much to say. And I'm sure you have a lot to tell us about all your experiences overseas."

How could she have known that was the last thing Jim wanted to talk about? In the years ahead, Jim never wanted to and never did talk about the war, even when asked. He would just change the subject. He wouldn't… couldn't… relive the horror.

Jim gave Irene a long, loving kiss and held her tightly. "I've missed you, Irene, and I've missed seeing my little girl grow up. Now that I'm home, I don't ever want to look back. I just want to be with the two of you here at home and never leave again."

"I've missed you, too, Jim," Irene said. "It's been hard trying to raise Meg alone. As you can see, she's a handful. And to make matters worse, your dad spoils her rotten. Every time I try to discipline her, he interferes or gets angry with me. I know he means well, but it just makes it that much harder for me."

While they collected the baggage and headed for the car, Meg tailed along behind, hugging her bear and her new doll, all but forgotten in her parents' reunion. On the way home, she insisted on sitting between them in the back seat of the big yellow Buick, her teddy and her beautiful new toy on her lap, listening to Les Brown's orchestra's "Sentimental Journey" playing scratchily on the radio and feeling a warm glow of happiness.

• • •

Things hadn't always been pleasant in her young life. When she was quite little, Meg had vague memories of moving a lot and never having many toys because it was hard to move too many things around all the time. At least that's what Irene always told her. She remembered once when she and her mother stayed in a cheap hotel for a while, the kind of hotel where a lonely man could always find a willing companion. The Senate Hotel was one of those places, loud and noisy. Laughter and music came from below almost every night. Irene constantly wanted her to take lots of naps and go to bed early, much too early for an active and curious child like Meg.

Little Meg would often hear music and laughter from the other room and wished she could join in the fun, too. Once, seeking attention, she decided to rebel, pretended to go to sleep, but instead swallowed four bobby pins out of spite. Irene had to rush Meg to St. Francis Hospital, where they took X-rays. They said she was going to be all right, but the doctors said she had to eat lots of mashed potatoes, graham crackers and, her least favorite of all, oatmeal, until she passed the bobby pins. Boy, she really caught hell from Irene for that little stunt after they got home.

"That's just like you, Meg O'Conner. You'll do anything to get attention. Well, I hope you like oatmeal, because you're going to be eating a lot of it for a long time." Irene was furious with her, not only because the hospital bill cost a lot of money, which she didn't have, but also because Irene didn't like unpleasant surprises in her life, especially when they came from Meg.

Meg was frequently left alone in her crib with just her teddy bear for company, her beloved soft Teddy with the yellow chenille legs. She had hugged him so much and so tightly that now he was all bent over in the middle. One time she remembered sharing him with another child that she didn't even know, and that was hard for her. Teddy was the one thing in her life that was all hers to have and to love, and she didn't want to share him with anybody.

When she was three, Meg had even been put into a Catholic orphanage for a few months. Meg hated it there. She missed her mother and feared the strict nuns. More than anything, she loathed all the oatmeal she had to eat. It seemed to be the main course on the menu. Meg was so short she couldn't get up into the tall beds at bedtime. The nuns would switch her on the backs of her small legs to "encourage" her to jump up into the bed. Meg would try not to scream and cry, but sometimes she just couldn't help it.

Eventually, she and her mother had moved in with Daddy's parents, a beneficial arrangement to both parties. Grandma Mary O'Conner had crippling arthritis and needed a lot of help around the house, and Irene needed a place to live. Life was happier for Meg then. The O'Conners were warm and caring Irish Catholics, and Meg flourished within the atmosphere of affection and love, fun, and laughter that filled their home.

She developed a special relationship with Grandpa Ryan, and he became her best buddy. They'd talk, laugh, take walks together, and share secrets. When she cried after being spanked by her mother, he was the one who comforted her, hugged her and wiped her tears. He'd hold her tight and rock her and say, "It's okay, honey, don't cry. Everything will be all right. I'm here now, so don't cry." Irene usually let her cry until she couldn't breathe any more or she threw up.

Meg remembered once when she'd lied to her mother about using her lipstick. Irene had found her favorite Tussy lipstick with the tip squished, the inside of the cap smeared with the dark red goo, when she went to apply it before leaving for her waitress job down at Angelo's Diner.

The moment Irene confronted Meg with the tube of lipstick, Meg started crying, backing up and shaking her head no. "Please, Mama, I didn't mean to do it. I just wanted to see how pretty I would look...." Irene's eyes flashed with fury as Meg kept screaming, "No...no, Mama. Please, I'll never do it again. Please!" She was pleading with her mother so loudly that Grandpa O'Conner heard her all the way downstairs.

Irene grabbed a wooden yardstick and beat her with it so hard it broke. As Meg sobbed in pain and fright, Irene glared at her and said, "That's what happens to bad little girls. And stop that crying. Stop it right now! It's not going to do any good, and nobody's going to pay any attention to you, anyway." When Meg couldn't stop, she advanced on her again, threatening, "You better stop crying right now, or I'll really give you something to cry about...."

Grandpa O'Conner came flying up the stairs and burst into the bedroom, his heart pounding at the sounds of his little Meg being beaten and pleading for mercy. When he saw what was happening, his face paled and then turned red. It was one of the few times Meg would ever see her grandfather get so angry.

"For God's sake, Irene, she's only a child of four!" he said as he caught Irene's arm midswing. "Children are curious and bound to get into things. She just wants to be like you, do what you do." His face was stern and red with fury as he told her, "I never want to see you hit her like that again, not while you're living in this house! And that's not a suggestion—that's an order!"

Irene was furious at the tongue-lashing. And she didn't appreciate his meddling in her affairs. After all, it was her kid. Irene hated having to live with the O'Conners, always interfering, watching her every move. But what other choice did she have? She couldn't make it on her own as a waitress, and somebody had to watch Meg while she was at work.

• • •

After Jim came home, things were happier for a little while. Irene was calmer and more content, less likely to find fault with Meg. Both of her parents worked to make ends meet, Irene as a waitress and her father at the shoe repair shop, but there never seemed to be enough money. Occasionally, Jim would have one of his recurrent malaria attacks and would have to stay home, shaking with fever. Meg was frightened and worried about her daddy, but Jim reassured her he would be fine, even though he had to talk through teeth that chattered from chills and high fever. Meg tried to help take care of him. She liked to help, and at least now she could see him, touch him, and be with him. He wasn't just a picture, he was real. Oh, how she loved him!

While Irene always seemed to resent Meg's presence, Jim liked to have her around, and often found pretexts for her to help him out with some chore. They'd do little projects together, and he would pretend she was invaluable to him. Once when he made a birdhouse for the front yard, he let her hammer two of the sides together. He held the wood and got the nails started, then she finished pounding them in.

Wanting perfection, tears welled up in Meg's eyes when she finished. "I'm sorry, Daddy. My side doesn't look as good as the side you made. I guess it's not a very good birdhouse," she said with a big, pouting lower lip.

Taking a step back, he studied the birdhouse intently, finger on chin. "For your very first birdhouse, Meg, it's a fine job. Besides, the little birdies won't notice if it's not absolutely perfect. They'll feel darn lucky and happy to have such a nice birdhouse this winter." They hugged and smiled, proud of their accomplishment. "Now what color should we paint it?"

The only time Irene seemed to like having her around was when her friends were over. She'd profess loudly how much she loved her beautiful little girl and would put her arm around Meg and hug her. Sometimes Meg just wanted to throw up when Irene did that. It was so phony.

Meg had very few toys, and most of her clothes were hand-me-downs, but since she'd never known any other way, she didn't mind. The family didn't go out much, due to lack of money and Grandma Mary's arthritis. Instead, they found pleasure in everyday enjoyments. Holidays were always special, and friends filled the house with laughter, congeniality, and wonderful holiday food and drinks.

The family made their own entertainment. Meggy always liked to sing with the radio. She knew most of the words to "Rum and Coca-Cola," and would sing that song especially loud and slightly off key.

At that, Jim would cover his ears and say to her, "Do you call that singing?" Then Meg would sing even louder and he'd press his hands to his head even tighter. This little game would go on until they were both hysterical with laughter.

Meggy loved sitting with the family in her grandparents' parlor in the evening listening to radio shows. Grandpa

O'Conner would open the doors on the large Philco console radio and Meg would race to his chair so she wouldn't miss out on her favorite seat—his lap. They'd tune in "The Jack Benny Show," "Fibber McGee and Molly," or "Amos and Andy." Meg would watch Grandpa closely and when he'd laugh, she'd laugh. Sometimes they'd just listen to the wonderful music of the big bands, songs like "My Dreams are Getting Better All The Time," and "Gotta Be This Or That" by Benny Goodman.

Meg had natural rhythm and loved to dance to the music with a lively beat. Her mom and dad would sometimes give her sips of their beer, laughing at her as she twirled and spun to the music until she got so dizzy she'd fall down, silly and giggling.

But slowly things began to change. Her mother became more and more critical of her again, ready to fly off the handle at any moment and for any reason. The natural curiosity of a child was Meg's enemy, and she always seemed to be in one kind of trouble or another. Irene seemed to look for things for her to do wrong. By the age of five, Meg had learned it was easier, not to mention safer, to deny and lie to avoid trouble with her mother. Meg was one of those unfortunate kids who, no matter what they did, always got caught. And Irene was always there, always ready to scold and punish her.

• • •

It was Christmas, that magical time of wonder and delight for a child, and a very special time at the O'Conner's. Even though Grandma O'Conner was bedridden, she'd read Christmas stories to Meg from her bed. This year Gramps had brought home some wallpaper remnants and Meg was carefully cutting out strips of paper from the prettiest designs. Grandma Mary was going to help her make paper chains from the scraps of fancy paper to decorate the tree.

On Christmas Eve they all gathered to listen to the holiday music on the radio. With childish trust and the hope of wonderful promises to come, Meg turned her shiny bright green eyes to the beautiful Christmas tree. She just knew Santa Claus would come that night with lots of special presents especially for her.

With a twinkle in his eye, Gramps lifted her up off his lap and told her, "Meg, would you go over and get that big present from under the tree? The one wrapped in the paper with the angels on it?"

Meg ran over and picked up the big box and brought it over to him.

He handed it back to her, saying, "Go ahead, open it now. This is a special present from Grandma Mary and me."

Meg gasped in surprise. A present to open now? She had to be the luckiest girl in the world. She carefully undid the tape on the beautiful package, wanting to save the pretty paper for some unknown use later. The red box was something she would keep, too. Lifting the lid, she slowly folded back the crisp white tissue paper.

Inside was a new pair of soft red flannel pajamas. There was lace at the cuffs, and shiny pearl buttons down the front. They were the most extravagant thing Meg had ever received. Grandpa and Grandma had bought them at Read's Department Store especially for her to wear to bed on Christmas Eve.

"Oh, Gramma, Gramps, they're so beautiful! My old ones were tight, and they had holes in the knees. Thank you! I just love them!" She hurled herself at them with hugs and kisses.

"Okay, Meg, time for bed," Jim said. "You run up and get ready, and we'll be right up to tuck you in."

Hugging her treasure to her chest, she kissed everyone good night and flew gaily up the stairs. She knew the sooner she got to sleep, the sooner Santa Claus would come. In her excitement to put on her beautiful new pajamas, she forgot to take off her patent leather shoes, and the buckles got caught in the ruffled lace cuffs and tore them. She looked down at her feet, aghast. Just then, Irene came into the room. Meg panicked and tried to hide her legs under the covers, but it was too late.

"Margret O'Conner! What have you done now? How could you be so careless? Those are expensive pajamas. Oh, you're always ruining something." With fire in her eyes, Irene seized Meg and dragged her toward the bathroom. "That's exactly why you never get anything new. You don't deserve nice things. You're just a careless, bad little girl." She bent Meg over her lap, pulled down the seat of the new pajamas and spanked her bare bottom with her big wooden hairbrush. Despite the happiness of the Christmas season, despite the joy and hope in a little girl's heart, her mother gave her a whipping on Christmas Eve.

2

Six-year-old Meg rushed breathlessly from room to room, opening closet and cupboard doors and sticking her head out the window to inspect the view. "Daddy," she called with excitement, "come look outside. You can see the garden from up here. We're up really high!"

She was very excited that they were moving into their very own apartment, but a little sad to be moving away from Grandpa and Grandma O'Conner's house. They always had such fun together. But then again, it would be nice to have her very own room to play in.

Her mother, tired of the incessant supervision of Jim's parents, had badgered Jim to move out of the elder O'Conners' house and find their own place. Acceding to

Irene's demands, Jim agreed, and finally they found an affordable apartment nearby on Douglas Street. The landlord had converted the old wooden house into two apartments, which were very small, but at least it was a place of their own, a place where Irene could have some privacy. There was no bathtub, so Meg bathed in a big washtub once a week (whether she needed it or not).

The rent was relatively inexpensive, but it was still a struggle for Irene and Jim. Irene was still working as a waitress, and Jim worked at the shoe repair shop. Most of their furniture was cast-offs and hand-me-downs from relatives, but Irene's folks have given them a big maroon mohair chair that was big and soft, and Meg loved to cuddle into it with her Teddy or her dad. She never noticed how threadbare it was, or how many moth holes it had.

Meg started first grade at St. Mary's Catholic School that fall, walking all the way across town alone every day. Irene felt that public school would be a bad influence on Meg, and so she'd enrolled her in Catholic school, hoping the nuns would be able to control her headstrong daughter and teach her to behave. Sometimes Meg got lost walking that far alone, but when that happened, she'd just go up to somebody's house and tell them who she was and where she lived, and they'd help her get home. Shyness was a stranger to Meg; she trusted everybody and figured everyone had a heart as innocent and loving as her own.

On her first day of school, Meg surreptitiously tiptoed into her mother's bedroom. She wanted to look extra pretty that day, so stood before the dresser mirror to put on a little bit of her mother's bright red lipstick. As she carefully replaced it in the drawer, her eyes alit on a little silver box. It had a card taped to the top with the words, "For Meg," on it. If this was for her, why was it in her mother's drawer?

She opened the lid. Inside was a delicate little locket and matching gold bracelet. She lifted the necklace out of the box and held it before her as she looked in the mirror. Oh, she looked so pretty. Quickly she clasped it around her neck and put on the bracelet. Now she would be the prettiest girl in the class.

Her first day of school was exciting and fun. She enjoyed being with the other children and loved the smell of the classroom, the papers, chalk dust and books. When her teacher passed out their textbooks, she quickly opened hers and buried her nose between the pages, savoring the fragrance of the new book.

At recess she climbed on the play equipment and skipped rope with some other girls. This was heaven!

Back inside class, to her horror, she discovered the golden bracelet was missing. She must have lost it during recess. The rest of the day lost its shining luster, and right after the bell rang, Meg ran to the playground and searched. It was gone. Maybe, she hoped against hope, her mother wouldn't notice.

At home that afternoon, Meg went to change into play clothes. When Irene came in to see how her day had gone, she saw the necklace around Meg's tiny throat.

"Where did you get that!" she said furiously. "You've been snooping in my drawers, haven't you?"

"But Mama, the box had my name on it, and I thought it was for me."

"That doesn't matter. You are never to go into my room, and never go into my drawers without permission." She angrily removed the necklace and held it in her hand. "Where's the bracelet?" she demanded.

Meg held her head down, unable to meet the flaring anger in her mother's eyes. "It got lost on the playground," she muttered.

"What? That does it! First you steal out of my room, and then you're so careless you lose something valuable. You don't deserve nice things, and that's one reason I never gave this to you." She had ahold of Meg's wrist and reached down and slapped her legs hard with her open hand. "Now get dressed and go sit in the living room."

Replacing the necklace in its box in her dresser, Irene's

mood softened, remembering the day she'd found the package with the exquisite little set inside on the front porch. On the box was the card that read, "For Meg." Irene clutched the box to her bosom.

Except for the strict nuns, whose stern visages and no-nonsense attitudes reminded her of her mother, Meg loved school. Knowledge was like food to her, and she devoured every scrap of learning she could get. The attention she received from her teachers for doing well inspired her to work even harder, and in some respects it made up for the lack of positive attention at home. She was very precocious, very bright, and open and friendly to everyone. On the rare occasions when she was reprimanded, it was usually for talking too much.

• • •

Meg went to the Kelvinator and carefully took out the long white box of flowers. Placing it on the red checkered oilcloth on the table, she lifted the lid to peek inside. Nobody had ever given her flowers before, but this was a very special day. It was May of 1949, and today was a momentous occasion in Meg's life—she was making her First Communion in the Catholic Church. Dressed in a ruffled, lacy white dress and veil, she felt like a beautiful grown-up lady. The lush bouquet of fresh daisies and tulips and her frilly white dress were presents from Gramps O'Conner.

He'd taken her shopping to Read's, the nicest store in town. "Entering the Church as a bride of Christ is an important event, Meg, and I'm very proud of you. You're a sweet and lovely little girl, and you know Grandpa and Grandma love you lots."

She was grateful Gramps had bought her the dress. The one her mother had wanted to buy wasn't nearly as nice. Last week her dad and mom had had another big fight because Jim had bought her a new pair of shoes for this special day. Irene had yelled and fought with him, throwing the shoes across the room in anger because he'd spent money on Meg without her permission. Whenever Meg needed anything—new shoes, something for church, something for school—there was always a big argument. Her new shoes had suffered a little dent in the heel, but Meg didn't care. They were still magnificent to her.

The ceremony at St. Mary's was glorious. Lines of girls in frilly white dresses, all carrying colorful bouquets of spring flowers and boys in white shirts and pants, filled the aisles, and the church was permeated with the fresh, sweet smell of the blossoms. Youthful heads bowed in devout prayer, immersed in the rituals that marked a rite of passage. Their clear young voices filled the immense church with chords of innocent praise. Meg felt a sense of awe, a oneness with the mystical strength of the Church and the Lord, linked to the precious power of God and her religion. She felt jubilant and important, and was proud to have her whole family there to share this meaningful day with her. It was an enchanting fantasy, marred only by the fact that her mother had insisted on cutting off her long braids and giving her a Toni home permanent two days ago, which had turned out frizzy. But no matter, her gossamer veil would cover most of the blonde fluff.

Back at home after the service, Irene told Meg, "Be sure you hang up your dress carefully. And don't use any of those wire hangers. Use the wooden one I gave you. I'm going to use some Rit and dye it blue tomorrow so you can use it for church on Sundays."

Meg changed into a play dress and carefully hung her exquisite white dress on the wooden hanger and put it in the closet. Her veil was carefully folded and placed in a special box on her closet shelf. Still aglow with happiness and the mystery of the timeless ceremonies, she wandered into the kitchen where Irene was preparing supper. Meg took one single daisy from her bouquet and pressed it between the pages of her Bible before putting the rest of the bouquet in a glass of water in the kitchen on the table.

"Mama," she asked, "would it be all right if I went downstairs and played with Debbie until dinner's ready? Mrs. Fickland is home from the hospital, and I want to see their new baby. Could I bring her and the baby a flower from my bouquet? Do you think she'd like that?"

The Ficklands were the landlords and lived in the downstairs apartment. Their daughter, Debbie, was a little younger than Meg, but the two girls liked to play together. Meg especially enjoyed visiting with Debbie because she had lots of toys and dolls to play with, and Meg had so few. She had her Teddy and one special doll with dark curly hair that she played with, and last Christmas she even got a doll buggy from Santa Claus. Debbie's mom sometimes made cute little outfits for Debbie's dollies on her Singer sewing machine out of fabric scraps left over from the dresses she made. Meg wished with all her heart that Debbie was her own sister so she'd have somebody to play with. Most of the time she felt so lonely, always being with adults.

Irene sighed and turned from the sink, wiping the back of her hand across her brow. Frowning, she said, "Oh, all right, Meg. Just be sure you mind your manners."

Meg went to the refrigerator and got an apple, then thoughtfully selected two flowers from the colorful bouquet to take to Debbie and her mother. As she hop-scotched down the stairs, she hummed to herself. The Fickland house was filled with pretty things, and Mrs. Fickland usually offered her a piece of candy from her carnival glass candy dish.

"Hi, Mr. Fickland," she said as the door opened. "Can Debbie play?" She looked up at her friend's daddy. He was a car salesman at the Studebaker showroom, and he always dressed nice, even on his day off. Sometimes Meg wondered what it would feel like if her daddy grew a thin pencil mustache, too. Would it tickle when he kissed her?

"Oh, hello, Meg, come on in. Debbie is taking a nap right now, and Mama and the baby have gone to visit her sister, but would you like to come in and play with the dolls until Debbie wakes up? It should be pretty soon now."

"I brought these flowers from my Communion bouquet for Mrs. Fickland and the baby," Meg offered, holding them out to him. "Aren't they pretty?" She hesitated at the doorway. She wanted to play with the dolls, and the hope of receiving some candy was a strong magnet. "I guess I can come in."

Meg entered and walked over to the play corner. She picked her favorite doll up out of the cradle and started fixing her long blonde hair. The doll looked a little bit like her, and it was Meg's favorite. Debbie's mother had even let her paint her doll's fingernails a beautiful bright red.

Leon came out of the kitchen with the flowers in a small bud vase. He put them on the coffee table, then came over and knelt on the floor beside her. He was a handsome man with a head full of jet-black hair and always wore Western shirts with shiny silver buttons and large belt buckles.

"These sure are pretty flowers. I know Mama and Debbie will like them. I'll bet you were the prettiest one today at your First Communion, all dressed in white like a beautiful little bride. Would you like a piece of candy from the dish as a Communion treat? I think we have some strawberry twists today."

He went over to the side table by the sofa and took out a piece of hard candy, patting the seat next to him. "Come on over here and sit next to me, honey, and tell me about everything that happened today. How many girls were there? Did you sing in the choir?"

A little shy about talking to Leon, but enticed by the candy that she seldom got at home, Meg put the doll back down in the cradle and walked over to the sofa and sat beside him. She carefully unwrapped the candy, put the paper in the ashtray, and began to suck on the sweet treat. Mr. Fickland put his arm around her and gave her a brief hug. Naturally affectionate, Meg leaned into his side. She craved kindness and needed love, always accepting hugs where she could get them.

"I bet you must be tired after such an exciting day," he said, stroking her hair. "It's nice and quiet right now, so why don't you put your head in my lap and take a little rest until Debbie wakes up?" He began to gently push her head down into his lap.

She rested quietly for a few moments while he stroked her hair gently like a little kitten and rubbed her back. Savoring the gentle, soft touches, Meg cuddled closer. Then Leon began stroking and rubbing her shoulders and arms. Gently he inched his hand farther down her body and slipped it into the tops of her white cotton panties.

Meg's eyes grew wide and she tried to sit up. She had never been touched there, except during bath time, and then only by her mother. Meg didn't know what, but something was terribly wrong and she was seized with anxiety. Mr. Fickland was breathing real loud, like he'd just run up a flight of stairs.

When he pulled her panties down, she panicked and tried to pull away. Her kicking knocked over the flowers on the table and the water spilled onto the rug.

"Please," she cried, pushing at his hands, "I have to go home now!"

He held her even tighter with his right arm and began to fondle her intimately, putting his fingers where it hurt. She cried and tried to twist away from him.

"Oh, that hurts! No! Please, don't!"

He held her head down hard in his lap, and cupped his hand over her mouth so her cries couldn't be heard. "Oh yes, you're so sweet, so sweet...." He began to moan softly.

Why was he doing this? He was hurting her! Meg was used to getting yelled at or getting a spanking, but this was a terrifying kind of pain. It made her feel bad in her heart. Meg began to choke from crying so hard and gasping for breath. Still he held her down while his fingers explored her roughly.

After an eternity, he finally let her go. She pulled away

from him and ran across the room, huddling in the corner. He got up off the couch and came over to her, offering her some more candy and some pennies, sweet-talking her to calm her down as he licked his lips and wiped the sweat from his face with his shirt sleeve.

"Now, Meg, that wasn't so bad. You're just such a pretty little thing that I couldn't help myself. All little girls like to be hugged and touched." Then his tone became harsh. "But you must never, ever tell your mother or father, or anyone else about this, because then they'll know you are a *bad* little girl. They'll send you away to an orphanage forever and you'll never see your parents again. Worst of all, God will punish you and you'll go straight to hell!"

Wide-eyed and terrified, gasping with sobs, she promised to keep quiet about what had happened, then ran out the door and up the stairs to her apartment. Jim and Irene were kneeling on the floor surrounded by tools and tubes, trying to fix the Motorola radio, and didn't pay any attention when she raced past them into her room.

"Meg, how many times have I told you not to run in here and slam the front door?" her mother yelled after her.

Alone in her room, she sobbed on her cot in the corner, guilty and frightened, ashamed and not knowing why. She hugged her soft yellow chenille teddy bear and wondered what to do. Maybe she *was* a bad little girl, but she would be better, she promised herself. She would never again use Mama's lipstick without asking, she would never tell another fib, and she would never sneak a piece of candy from the Ficklands' candy dish again. She would help Mama more, and would never, ever talk in school.

Meg prayed to God to forgive her for being such a bad little girl. What was she going to do? She couldn't tell her mom or dad or anybody. She felt desperately alone. In her innocent, childish way, she found a solution. She created a guardian angel for herself, someone who would protect and take care of her. After that, her angel, Delby, went everywhere with her. She would talk to him at night and tell him her innermost thoughts and secrets. At school she would sit way over on one side of her desk seat so Delby would have room to sit with her. When Sister Simone asked why she was crowded all the way to one end of the seat, she replied, "So there's room for Delby, my angel."

Meg was frightened to go downstairs to play with Debbie again and seldom did so any more, and only when she was sure Mrs. Fickland would be at home. Leon acted as if nothing had happened. He was friendly, but didn't try to come near her. But each time he smiled at Meg, she shuddered and remembered the pain. There was an ugly feeling in the pit of her stomach, a knot of fear and loathing that she felt was her fault. Maybe he'd just gone crazy for a little while, she thought. He didn't look like a mean man. Maybe it would be all right from now on.

Occasionally her mother left her with the Ficklands when she had to work and there was nobody else to take care of Meg. That November Irene had found a new job at Read's Department Store downtown on Stephenson Street, and with the Christmas season approaching, she sometimes had to work different shifts.

Irene was getting ready for work, adjusting her hat and the seams on her stockings. "Meg, get your crayons and that new coloring book and let's go. I can't be late for work today. Mrs. Fickland is going to babysit you until Daddy gets home."

Meg begged tearfully, "No, Mama, no. Please don't go to work. Can't I go with you? Oh, please? Can I go over to Grandpa's house instead?"

Irritated at her irrational and intense behavior, Irene angrily said, "Stop it, Meg! Stop it right now! You know I have to go to work, and you have to go downstairs, so quit acting like that this right this instant."

Cringing inside, Meg did as she was told. Debbie was happy to see her friend, and once she got there Meg began to relax a little. Debbie's mother was there, so everything should be all right.

"Leon, I'm going to run over to that big new market. Is there anything you need? Girls, you just play quietly. Debbie, your dad is working on some new ads for the dealership and needs to think. That's a good girl," she smiled.

Meg cringed in terror. With a haunted look, her eyes darted around the room. She had nowhere to hide. "Please, can't we go with you?" she pleaded with Mrs. Fickland.

"Not this time, honey. You girls have fun, and I'll bring you a treat when I come back."

The thought of staying there with Leon sent cold shivers all the way down Meg's spine. But what could she do? She felt somewhat safer since Debbie was there with them. She shrugged her little shoulders and decided she would just have to watch his every move.

Meg and Debbie played with paper dolls while Leon worked on his ads. After a while, he put down his pencil and stretched. "Debbie, it's about time for your afternoon nap. You girls have been playing a long time, and you both must be tired. Debbie, you go on into your bedroom and snuggle up, and be real quiet so you don't wake up the baby. Meg, you can rest right here on the couch. I think I'm going to take a little nap, too, before dinner." He squeezed Meg's shoulder and turned to go into his bedroom.

Meg's fears were slightly allayed. If he was asleep, he couldn't hurt her. Besides, Debbie would be right in the next room. As Leon turned to go into the bedroom, he turned to Meg and said, "Go ahead, Meg, just rest on the couch until Mrs. Fickland gets back from the market or until your mother gets home."

Meg was unsure about this, but she'd been taught to obey her elders. Besides, if he was going in the bedroom, he wouldn't be out here to bother her. She dragged her feet over to the sofa and slowly sat down, watching him cautiously for any suspicious moves. Like a frightened deer, she was ready to leap to any part of the room.

When he went into his bedroom and softly pulled the

door closed, she felt a lot safer. In her heart she knew she was in a dangerous predicament, but maybe he really was going to take a nap. Surely big people got tired, too. Just to make sure, she wouldn't sleep, she'd just rest a little while. Mama would be back soon and then she'd be safe in her own room.

She propped herself up against the fringed cushions on the Ficklands' flowered sofa facing the bedroom door. It was soft and comfortable, and the apartment was cozy and warm. Much against her will, her sleepy eyelids slowly began to close. Her little body trembled every once in a while as she started to drift off, and soon she was sound asleep.

• • •

She dreamed she was in a field of flowers, the benevolent sun warming her face, a soft breeze tickling the leaves on the trees. She lay tranquilly on a cushiony mat of woven grasses and leaves, feeling good to be alive. A tiny brown bunny, hesitant and shy, crouched near her outflung hands, its downy fur grazing her fingertips. Her breathing was slow and steady now as her little body sunk peacefully into the cushions.

"Oh, what a cute little bunny," she whispered in her sweet dream, and cuddled it next to her cheek. She'd always wanted a pet, but her mother said she couldn't have one in the apartment. Of course, that didn't stop stray animals from "following" Meg home from school. A little coaxing on Meg's part didn't hurt, either. But Irene's answer was always the same.

"You know you can't keep it, so just take it back to wherever you found it. Animals are messy and smelly and have fleas. Besides, there's barely enough room and food for all of us in this little apartment, let alone some animal."

Meg did as she was told, crying all the way. She knew these lost little animals needed someone to love them and take care of them, and Meg had a large space in her warm heart that overflowed with love for these abandoned creatures. They needed her as much as she needed them. But Irene wouldn't let her have a pet.

● ● ●

As she caressed the soft, velvety bunny fur in her dream, she became aware of another sensation. Something was rubbing against her legs. In a panic, her eyes flew open. Her little body stiffened and she yelled, "NO! Please, no! Don't! I don't like it! Please, don't!" Her screams stuck in her throat and only choked whimpers came out.

"Just lie still, honey. I only want to show you how much I like you. You're such a pretty little girl, so young and fresh." His breath was hoarse and ragged and he was sweating as he rubbed his hands along the insides of her legs, moving them rapidly up to her panties.

Quickly, he yanked them down and spread her legs open. "I have to look and see if you're nice and clean. If you're not, I can wash you. You'd like that, wouldn't you, Meg?"

"Oh no, please stop," Meg pleaded. "I'm clean. I just had a bath last night. I'm clean. Please…." Meg inhaled her sobs and twisted in a frenzy to escape.

"You be quiet now," he panted. "You're just so pretty and pure and young…." He began to push his fingers into her, holding her down with his other arm and kissing her small squirming face, a face streaked with tears.

She couldn't see what was happening, but it hurt. Suddenly, she felt a fierce pain and screamed aloud. She twisted under his arm to see him pushing the handle of a hairbrush into her. To stifle her screams, he clamped his hand over her mouth. Meg twisted and writhed in agony. He was unable to hold her down and keep her quiet at the same time, and Meg wrenched out of his grasp and ran for the door. She kept tripping with her panties around her ankles, but she had to get out of there. She heard her panties rip, but just kept tugging on them and running.

Alone in her apartment, she washed herself with a washcloth again and again in the sink, but couldn't feel clean. She hid her torn panties way at the back of her closet under a pile of old clothes so nobody would find them.

What had she done to deserve this? She felt so dirty, so soiled. Surely everyone who looked at her would know. What was she going to do? Should she tell God? Never mind. He knew. He knew what a bad little girl she was. Everyone knew! And boy, would she ever get a whipping if her mother found those torn panties. She ran to the closet and searched for the panties, taking them quickly to her doll buggy and stuffing them down in the bottom. Her mother never looked there, and she could tell her friends they were just rags.

When Irene got home from work, she was furious with Meg for not staying at the Ficklands' apartment like she was supposed to.

"Margret O'Conner, you're in big trouble now. You know you're not old enough to stay in this apartment all alone. I pay good money to have the Ficklands watch you while I work. You just won't mind, will you? You must never, ever do this again, or you'll be sorry. Do you hear me, missy?" When Meg remained mute, she raised her voice and yelled, "You better answer me right this minute!" Irene slammed the blue bowl with the picture of Shirley Temple in the bottom from the movie *Curly Top*, down on the table so hard it nearly broke. "Answer me!"

"Yes, Mama," Meg whispered, looking at her shoes. Her fear of Leon Fickland gave her the courage to speak up. "But, Mama, I'm...I'm afraid."

"Afraid? Afraid of what? Let me tell you something. You'll really have something to be afraid of if you ever do anything like this again!"

Meg was quiet for a while, but then the truth burst out. "He hurt me, Mama. Every time I go down to play with

Debbie, whenever me and him are all alone, he makes me lie down and then he takes off my panties and grabs me and touches me and pokes me. It hurts! It hurts me, Mama. He told me never to tell you because you would send me to an orphanage far away and I'd never see you or Daddy again." She was trembling with fright, guilty and ashamed and not knowing why, afraid of what her mother was going to say or do.

Her mother knelt in front of her and dug her steely fingers into Meg's small shoulders. "What did you say?" she asked in a fierce voice. "What kind of a story is that? How dare you tell such horrible lies about Mr. Fickland? You're going to get us in trouble with him, and then we won't be able to stay here. Do you want us to have to move? What would we do then?" Irene shook her until her curls flew back and forth. "You should be ashamed of yourself, Margaret O'Conner, for making up such a terrible thing. You go to your room right this minute, and I'll deal with you later. And don't you ever say a word to anyone about this again, especially not to your father."

As her daughter ran to her room, for just the briefest moment Irene reflected on how Meg had suddenly become so modest, refusing to be seen naked or accept any assistance with her bath. Could it possibly be true? Of course not. It was just Meg's overactive imagination, or some story she'd made up to keep from getting in trouble.

Meg was punished for lying and for jeopardizing their relationship with the landlord. Her mother didn't believe her, or didn't want to believe her. And Meg knew if her own mother didn't believe her, no one else would, either.

The next time Mr. Fickland tried again, however, Meg stood up to him. "You better leave me alone. I'm going to tell my daddy and my grandpa about you. They love me and they won't send me away. They won't like what you're doing. It's mean and it's wrong. It hurts me real bad. Even if I do get punished, even if they do send me away, I'm going to tell them! You're not going to hurt me again!"

And so the molestations stopped.

   She wondered why her mother hadn't believed her.
Why would she make up a horrible story like that? Somehow, at seven, Meg knew that something had been taken
away from her, something she could never get back. No
matter how good she tried to be, there was something bad
about her. Although she vowed never to tell a single person
what had happened to her, she still felt everyone always
knew just by looking at her face. They all knew.

3

"Jim, hurry up and get that table in here! The rain will ruin the finish," Irene called from the stairs as she trudged up with another box of household belongings.

Jim swore softly under his breath as he hefted the bedside table in his arms. He'd gotten some friends to help move the furniture, but moving was still a lot of hard work, and he was getting tired and grumpy.

It was pouring down rain that April day in 1951 when Meg and her family moved into their big new apartment on the other side of town, but not even the rain could dampen nine-year-old Meg's joy. The house on Chicago Street was only a block and a half from Saint Mary's, so she would have no more long walks to choir practice, school and church. Best of all, no more Leon Fickland. Meg was ecstatic. The neighborhood was more respectable, and she was happy there were children her age in the neighborhood for her to play with.

Meg ran around enthusiastically, exploring her new surroundings. She opened doors and looked in closets, squinted through the glass doorknobs to see if she could see a rainbow, then ran into the bathroom.

"Daddy, come look at this tub! It looks like a lion crouching here, with those claw feet on the bottom. And what's that?"

Jim looked at the mechanism hanging on the wall above the tub. "That's a water heater, Meggy. Every time you want to take a bath, I'll have to light that so you'll have hot water." And so he did on each and every Saturday night.

Although their upstairs apartment in the old brick building was bigger than their last place, it was still very old-fashioned. The wallpaper was of faded damask roses, and the wooden floors were old and dark. They were lucky, though. The kitchen had been remodeled and had a smooth linoleum floor and polished hardwood counter tops. There were even working gas jets in the walls for lights. The only problem with the place was that in the attic above them they could hear squirrels skittering around at night, and sometimes Irene saw bats flying in and out through the tiny broken dormer window.

One evening after dinner when Meg was helping her mother with the dishes, Irene saw something flap into the window. "A bat!" she shrieked. "It'll get in my hair! Jim, help! Get this awful thing out of here!" Meg and her mother frantically flapped at it with newspapers, but that only confused the creature and caused it to career even more frantically in the small room. The women of the house shrieked and ran for cover.

"Shoo! Shoo, you ugly thing!" Her father picked up the broom and came running to the rescue. "Open that other

window, Meg, and maybe I can make it fly out that way."
He swatted at the animal with wild swings.

Meg hurriedly opened the window wide and crouched
on the floor with a sheet of newspaper over her head so the
bat wouldn't get in her hair. When the confused bat turned
in flight and flew straight for her, Irene shrieked and
dropped to the floor.

Jim, in his boxer shorts, became their knight in shining
armor. While Meg and her mother cowered in the corner in
terror, their faces streaked with newspaper-blackened tears,
Jim cut a heroic figure, swatting at the bat with a broom to
get it to fly out the window.

"You girls just stay right where you are. I'll get it out
of here." Bumping into chairs and tables, he chased the
small black creature through the kitchen until it acciden-
tally found the open window and disappeared into the
night.

With the beast safely gone, he turned and, hitching up
his underwear and brandishing his broom, exclaimed,
"Aha, fair maidens. You can come out now, 'tis safe with
the dragon banished. But I must say," he added with a
laugh, "with that black stuff streaked all over your faces,
you girls look a little like bats yourselves."

The best part about being in the new apartment was that
her beloved Grandpa Ryan O'Conner, her best buddy,
came to live with them. Grandma Mary had died a year ago,
and he was no longer able to live alone. Gramps would play
checkers and gin rummy with her, and they still listened to
the radio programs together in the evenings.

Their long walks taken hand-in-hand were special
moments that Meg treasured. He was never too busy to
make time for her, and no question was too small for him
to consider a reply. Meg loved the closeness and joy that
Gramps brought to the family. No matter what, he could
always make Meg believe that nothing was ever that bad
and that everything would be all right.

It was about a week before her tenth birthday, and Meg

and her grandpa were working on a puzzle on the kitchen table. Meg seemed unusually quiet and a little sad and he could tell there was something bothering her.

"You look like Droopy, that sad-eyed dog character, Meg. Is there something bothering you that you'd like to talk about?"

She heaved a sigh and propped her chin into her hand, elbow on the table. A couple of months ago her best friend, Cindy, had turned ten, and her mother had put on a small birthday party for her, inviting six girls to come. They had played Pin The Tail On The Donkey and Blind Man's Bluff, and Cindy's mom had made a big chocolate cake and decorated it with writing that said, "Happy Birthday, Cindy." Oh, it had been so much fun.

Meg had to argue with her mother about getting to go, since Irene didn't want to spend the money on a present. Jim wanted her to go. Meg didn't have enough fun in her life, he argued, and Cindy was a nice girl in the neighborhood, from a good family. In the end, they had compromised, and Meg had carefully wrapped up her favorite copy of *Little Women* to give her as a gift. It was just like new. Meg always took good care of whatever she got.

With a wistful sigh, she turned to her favorite friend. "Gramps," she said hopefully, "do you think it would be okay if I asked Mama if I could have a couple of my friends over for my birthday? It would just be Mary Taylor and Cindy Sullivan. They're really nice girls, and I know she'd like them. We wouldn't have to have a party or a cake or anything, and we'd play real quietly in my room. Maybe they could even spend the night."

Her mother sometimes let her go overnight to Cindy's house, but Meg had never had a slumber party at her house. Irene never even made the effort to have Meg's school friends over to play. When Meg would ask, Irene would reply, "Oh, Meg, you know I'm too busy. Besides, our apartment is too small and a bunch of girls over here would be too disruptive and they'd be in the way."

Meg had never had a birthday party because her mother thought parties were too much work and didn't like children messing up her house.

After their move, Irene seemed to be sick a lot and took a lot of pills. She was in the hospital more than she was at home, and when she was at home, she seemed to stay in bed most of the time with one of her headaches. Meg had grown up quickly, taking over the responsibilities of the woman of the house in their new place. At the tender age of nine, Meg had learned to cook, clean, wash clothes in the old Maytag wringer machine, and take care of the family. Her mother was always complaining that she didn't get things clean enough. Maybe she didn't do it well, but everything got done.

Meg didn't mind that much. With the radio playing softly in the background, a too-big apron tied around her slim waist, she would hum along with Dinah Shore as she went about her chores. Pushing the carpet sweeper, she'd pretend she was married to a rich, handsome man and that she was the most beautiful girl in the world.

She imagined her beautiful children playing in the other room and thought about how much she'd love them and play with them and have fun with them. She'd never be too busy. She'd never be mean to them. She'd have parties for them and take them on trips to the zoo and the swimming pool. Of course, her daughter would have dance lessons and piano lessons, and her son would be an excellent baseball player, playing with his handsome dad on weekends while they picnicked in the park.

Grandpa Ryan put down the puzzle piece he was holding and turned to her with a sad look on his face. Forcing a happy look, he took her small hand into his large bony grasp. "Oh, I don't think your mother would approve of that, honey. But what do you say we walk down to Roy's and get an ice cream soda instead? And I'll buy a present especially for you. You pick out anything you like."

Meg squealed with delight. "A toy? A book? A new doll dress for Alice? Anything?"

"Anything your heart desires, princess. But first, I'd better check and see what the moths in my wallet have to say about that," he said with a chuckle.

The smile returned to her sunny face, and she rushed around the table to give this loving man a bone-crushing hug.

• • •

It was Meg's first day in fourth grade at St. Mary's, and she was looking forward to it. She wanted to look extra special pretty this morning. Hitching up her too-long, hand-me-down cotton slip with a piece of twine, she rolled it up to the right length. Quickly she got down her pleated blue skirt and a crisp white blouse, the St. Mary's school uniform. Mary Jane shoes went onto her feet with white ankle socks. A big bow tied back her long, silky ash-blonde hair.

She made a striking picture in the bathroom mirror, and even the plain school uniform couldn't hide her extraordinary beauty. She washed her face and went in to make herself some breakfast. Dad had already left for work, and Gramps was still sleeping. Irene was sleeping soundly, as usual. After she ate a breakfast of Wheaties and milk and a glass of orange juice and washed her dishes, she was almost ready.

Quietly, she slipped into her mother's room, trying not to awaken her. The pull shades were drawn, and her mother did not stir. Meg quietly tiptoed over to Irene's jewelry box and opened the lid. Carefully, she selected a necklace with earrings and bracelet to match.

Meg would sometimes borrow pieces of Irene's costume jewelry, wearing the gaudy, outrageous stuff to school. Everybody laughed at her, but she didn't care. It made her feel older and prettier. Not many other girls wore rhinestones in the fourth grade.

Meg enjoyed school and did well, her precocious

nature and perpetual curiosity providing the means to get good grades. But she didn't have many school friends. She was different, grown up beyond her years, dressed in her funny hand-me-down clothes.

That morning as she walked proudly into the school building, the older girls turned to stare at her and some started to giggle.

"Get a load of that jewelry. I wonder if her mother knows she's wearing it," whispered one of them. A few of the fifth and sixth grade girls gave her looks of deep animosity. Meg didn't know why. She didn't even know them. Older girls were jealous of her striking beauty, even at her young age.

● ● ●

In fifth grade, her favorite teacher at St. Mary's was Sister Augustus. Most of the other nuns were strict and stern. Oh, they were honest and fair, but not someone Meg could feel close to. Sister Augustus taught them well, but she was also sweet, gentle, and incredibly kind, with the face of an angel.

Meg hurried along through the mushy snow, carrying a brown paper bag full of valentines she and Gramps had worked on last night. She'd made each and every one of them herself, using pieces of construction paper, a few doilies, and scraps from the wallpaper books she had in her room.

This Valentine's Day morning she was meeting Sister Augustus early in class to help her clean the boards and set up for the party they were having that day. She liked the quiet mornings she shared with the loving nun, who always had time for her. Unlike her mother, Sister Augustus listened to Meg, and they spent many mornings together, just talking about things Meg was curious about. Sister Augustus gave her the loving acceptance and quiet conversations that she missed at home.

Because of her, Meg had even seriously considered becoming a nun, having long talks with Sister Augustus and Father Murphy about entering the convent. It seemed like such a quiet, serene, and peaceful way of life, a life free from ridicule and criticism. In the convent, she could have a life of peace, beloved by her Savior, away from the sadness she'd known too much of in her young life.

"Sister Augustus," she said, interrupting the older woman from her work, "I...I don't think the other girls like me very much. Hardly anybody ever asks me over to play after school, and most of them don't seem very nice to me."

The nun put down the pen she was correcting papers with and came over to give Meg a hug. She knelt so they were at eye level. "You know, Meg, sometimes children can be more cruel to other children than anybody else. They make fun of anybody and anything that's a little bit different than they are. Why, the other kids used to make fun of me when I was your age because I wore glasses and had red hair. They used to call me 'Four-Eyes' and would chant a silly thing like, 'Redhead, redhead, fire in the woodshed.' It sounds silly, but it hurt my feelings."

She paused and lifted Meg's chin up so she could look directly into her eyes. "But each and every person is different and has special qualities that make them who they are. You always remember that. You're a wonderful, sweet girl, and you are special just the way you are." She felt sorry for this sweet, lonely little child.

Meg nodded her head in understanding. Sister Augustus could always make her feel better, and most of the time what she said was right. But she knew that part of what Sister Augustus said to her wasn't entirely true. The kids at school were sometimes mean and made fun of her, but they weren't cruel...not like her mother could be.

•••

Meg clutched the beautiful white Easter lily in her

hand, wrapped with a piece of rag and tin foil to keep it fresh and pretty. She was bringing it to Sister Augustus for the vase on her desk. The flower reminded her of the upcoming season of Lent and celebration, bringing the promise of rebirth and salvation. It was a time of year she always loved.

As she neared the school, she noticed a group of girls gathered near the front door of the big brick building. They were whispering in excited tones, and one or two of them were crying.

Seeing her friend, Cindy Sullivan, Meg hurried over to see what was the matter. "What's the matter, Cindy? Why are you crying?"

"Oh, Meg, it's just awful," moaned her friend. "When we got to school this morning, Mother Superior told us that last night Sister Augustus passed away. Something about her heart…." Cindy burst into tears and hugged her friend.

Meg's knees gave out on her, and she had to sit down quickly on the steps. No. No, Sister Augustus couldn't leave her. She couldn't. Her heart felt as if someone had put an icy-cold iron band around it and attached a heavy weight. The sense of loss and betrayal Meg felt was immense. The only woman close to her had left her, and now part of her life was an empty void.

The funeral was set for two days later, and the whole school attended. But it was Meg who cried loudest and longest, her young heart sobbing for the loss of the loving woman who was her friend.

4

Meg sat on the brick stoop of their apartment house, enjoying the feel of the warm sun on her skin and staring up at the blue September sky. Her head tilted back so that her long, thick blonde hair cascaded down her back, she watched the clouds, picking out shapes and pretending she was a bird, soaring free in the sky in the sunlight.

With a smile, she got up and headed downtown to Woolworth's to do her errands. She had to buy notebook paper and pencils and other supplies for school next week, and her mother wanted her to get some new dish towels and a package of butter mints and a tin of Planter's Spanish peanuts for her card club today. And if there was any change left over, Irene had said she could get some Beech-nut gum.

At twelve, Meg was maturing into a beautiful girl with the inevitable questions and concerns about growing up. Her developing body was a mystery to her, and she was beginning to have feelings about boys that she didn't fully understand. Her emotions bounced from one end of the spectrum to the other, sometimes within a matter of minutes. One moment she was elated just to be alive, exhilarated by the sensations of the warm sun on her skin, the breeze caressing her hair, surrounded by the sweet scents of the living earth. Other times she felt sad and depressed for no reason at all. Lately, she'd even been grumpy with her beloved Gramps, and she felt ashamed of herself.

At Woolworth's, in addition to the school supplies, she spent some time in the cosmetics section. Meg was starting to experiment with make-up and becoming more interested in her appearance. She had a little money from babysitting the little girl across the street, and old Mr. Stewart had given her a dollar for washing his windows last Saturday. Irene encouraged her to work, saying, "Oh, let her, Grandpa Ryan. She needs to know where a dollar comes from."

Meg hoped she had enough money for everything she wanted. She was shopping for three items in particular for herself today. First and foremost, she wanted a tube of Tanjee lipstick, the kind that changed color when you put it on. It didn't get very dark, but it turned a nice pink that she didn't think her mother would notice too much. Secondly, she was looking for a little bottle of Paris Midnight cologne. It came in a pretty blue bottle and had a picture of the Eiffel Tower on the front. Someday, she'd be able to afford good perfume, like her mother used.

She picked up a bottle Femme Fatale crimson nail polish. She'd have to sneak it into her room so that her mother wouldn't find out. Whenever she put it on, she felt so exotic and grown up. But it never lasted long. She'd always have to chew it off before she came back home. She didn't know what her mother would do if she found out she was wearing nail polish.

On her way back home, she felt an uncomfortable moistness between her legs. She didn't have to go to the bathroom, so wondered what it could be. Her panties felt really wet. Oh well, it was a hot day, and she was sweating a lot. It was a long walk downtown and back. She'd change when she got back home.

"Hello, Mrs. Taylor, Mrs. Sullivan," Meg greeted the two ladies who were already there, sipping coffee. "Here's your mints and nuts, Mama."

"Did you get the towels like I asked you?" Turning to her friends, Irene complained, "Half the time she forgets what I asked her to get." The ladies smiled uncomfortably.

"Yes, Mama, they're right here," Meg replied with a sigh, handing her the brown paper bag. "And the change is in the bag, too." She was embarrassed that her mother would critcize her like that in front of her friends.

Meg went into her bedroom and examined her treasures. She'd hide her new cosmetics under the blanket in her doll buggy. It was her favorite hiding place. Although she never played with dolls any more, she still kept her old doll, Alice, and the buggy in a corner of her room.

Getting out a fresh pair of panties and a clean pair of shorts, she headed for the bathroom. She'd take a quick bath and put her hair up in a ponytail, too. Maybe that would cool her off a little bit. In the bathroom, she stripped off her damp clothing and was getting out fresh towels and the baby powder for after her bath when she noticed the blood on her underwear. She was bleeding! Oh, God, she was dying!

"Mama!" she called, "Mama, help!"

Her mother stuck her head in the door to the bathroom. "What is it, Meg? You know I'm busy right now."

Meg pointed to her underwear. "I'm bleeding, Mama. Something's wrong with me. I must be dying! What am I going to do?"

Irene looked at the underwear, then at her daughter, and then burst out laughing. Meg couldn't understand what was so funny. She was dying, and her mother was laughing.

"Oh, Meg, you're not dying. You've just got 'The Curse.' You've got your period."

Meg had heard some of her friends talking about their periods, but didn't really understand what they were talking about. Her mother sat on the edge of the claw-footed bathtub and explained to her briefly what to do. From the cabinet beneath the bathroom sink she produced the necessary supplies and showed her how to use them. The belt and pad were uncomfortable, and Meg didn't like it. She didn't want to wear shorts now because she felt like everybody could see what she had on underneath them, so asked her mother to go to her room and bring her a skirt.

"Every month now, Meg, you'll have to take care of yourself. That's where I keep my supplies, so you'll know where to find them." She explained how to wrap everything up carefully and hide it in the bottom of the trash receptacle. "You know, you can get pregnant now. Just be sure you don't let a man touch you down there." And that was the extent of her sex education.

Alone in the bathroom, Meg sat on the closed toilet seat lid, contemplating the changes that had happened today. From the living room, she could hear laughter. She fixed her ponytail and opened the bathroom door to go back to her room.

"...and she thought she was dying!" came her mother's voice from the living room. More laughter followed. Meg was mortified! It was a most private and emotional event, and her mother was in there, telling her card club friends all about it! She burst into tears and ran to her room, throwing herself onto the chenille bedspread.

• • •

"Hurry up, Meg, we're leaving," her mother called.

After they moved into the new apartment, even though they still didn't seem to have much money, her mom and dad started going to the Moose Club halfway across town almost every night after work, and they took her with them. It was a fraternal organization that did community work in the town, and they also had social events and dances for the members.

Meg rolled over on her cot, *Screenplay* movie magazine in hand. "Aw, Mama, do I have to go tonight? I can stay here with Gramps and just read. Wouldn't that be okay?"

"Your grandfather goes to bed early, and he doesn't need you making noise around him all the time. Besides, I never know what you'll do when we're away from home and you're all alone." Irene didn't seem to trust her, but Meg had never given her any reason not to.

Once they got there, Meg settled into her usual booth in the corner, with a vanilla Coke and her magazine before her. The Moose Club was a lively place, filled with lively people, and Meg usually liked going there. Most of them were her parents' age, but she loved being with people, and especially loved listening to the music on the jukebox. Sometimes they even had a live band. Tonight, though, she just wanted to be at home by herself.

Her dad slid in beside her. "How's tricks, princess?" He sipped on his beer and scanned the crowd, looking for Irene. Not seeing her, and noticing that Meg looked a little bored, he put down his beer and stood up before her. With great gravity, he bowed low before her. "My lady, wouldst thou honor me with thy presence for this dance?" They were playing an old tune, "Stardust," one of his favorites.

Meg loved to dance with her dad, whirling and waltzing, twirling and spinning. He was handsome and tall, and moved with grace and poise.

"Why yes, gentle knight, this lady wouldst be honored to dance with thou. But only if you promise not to step on my feet," she joked.

She moved easily into his arms on the dance floor. No one danced like Jim O'Conner. Tall for her age, Meg was able to keep up with his long, graceful steps and beautiful turns, her eyes half closed, lost in the music. She imagined herself a princess, dancing with her prince in *"Snow White."*

Suddenly she could feel a pair of malevolent eyes on her back. She opened her own eyes and looked around, trying to see who was staring at her so balefully. There was a look on her mother's face that made her feel uncomfortable and scared.

Meg wondered why her mother seemed so angry with her when she danced with her dad, since Irene spent most of her time dancing with all the other men. She hardly ever danced with Jim, even though in Meg's estimation her dad was the best dancer there.

Usually, Meg found herself sitting alone at a table in the corner of the Moose Club bar room, trying to do her homework. It was hard to study with the jukebox or bands playing every night, and her grades were starting to go down a little. Each night she'd work for as long as she could, and then she'd fall asleep with her head on her books or cradled in the crook of her arm. Her parents had to wake her up to walk home again late at night, as they still didn't have a car of their own. On winter nights, that late, long walk was agony, shivering in the freezing cold with the deep snow crunching underfoot.

Sometimes Meg dreamily wished that there were a special someone her age there at the Moose Club that she could dance with to the songs she loved—"Because of You" by Tony Bennett; the McGuire Sisters harmonizing on "Teach Me Tonight," and that old favorite, "Mr. Sandman." Most of her education that year was in the school of life, watching people get drunk, flirt, dance and laugh at the Moose Club.

Everyone in the club liked Jim, and Jim liked everyone. Eventually, both her parents had held most of the offices in the fraternal order. It was a major part of their lives, and most of their friends and social life centered around the organization.

In addition to the dances, the club sponsored lots of other activities. In the summer there were picnics and corn boils held in the wooded areas outside of town. While the grownups ate and drank too much, Meg and her teenage friends would sneak into the woods and play kissy-kissy games.

One boy in particular, Steve Workman, was always after Meg. It was the first time a boy had ever shown any interest in her and she was immensely flattered. She loved the attention and liked the feeling of being needed, but she never let things go too far. Her young blood would flow hot after heavy necking, but she could never forget the pain between her legs from a few years ago and always stopped it before it was too late. It was exciting, and it felt good to have somebody love her—to a point.

• • •

The Moose Club was having its annual holiday party and dance early in December that year, and Meg really didn't want to go, but her parents had made her go with them, anyway. There was nobody her age there, she was exhausted from school work and getting ready for the Christmas dance at St. Mary's, and she just wanted to stay home and get some sleep. She couldn't find her mother, and reluctantly Jim said it would be all right for her to walk home alone.

"Just be sure you walk fast and stay on the lighted streets, honey. And don't talk to any strangers on the way home. I'll come kiss you good night when we get back, okay?"

Their new apartment was larger and had two bed-rooms, but when Grandpa O'Conner had moved in with them, Meg had given her bedroom to her beloved best friend. She and Gramps shared the closet and a dresser in the bedroom, but she slept in the dining room on a rollaway bed, a bed whose linens seldom got changed and always smelled of body oils and odors. Although her mother was seldom in the hospital any more, she still did very little around the house, and so it was up to Meg to perform the cleaning, cooking, and laundry. Meg had so many other daily chores, it was hard for her to keep up with them all.

When Meg got home from the party, she peeked in on her Grandpa, who was snoring lightly in his sleep. Wearily she tiptoed over to her dresser and got out a nightgown, carefully hanging up her lavender wool slim skirt. She folded her white orlon sweater and put it on top of the dresser and unhooked the angora fake collar she'd worn to complete the outfit. She put her books on top of the dresser, too, and kissed Gramps softly before she left the room. Going to the bathroom, she conscientiously brushed her teeth and washed her face and then slid beneath the welcome soft, if not clean, sheets of her little cot. The dim light from the bathroom cast a comforting glow down the hallway.

She was almost asleep when she heard the front door creak open. It must be her parents finally getting home. They were both drunk, or pretty far gone, anyway. Meg didn't make a sound, pretending she was asleep so she wouldn't have to deal with them in that condition. She had been through enough unpleasant scenes with her mother when Irene was in her cups.

The two adults bumped and staggered noisily into the living room and turned the radio on softly, then went to the kitchen to fix themselves a couple more drinks. Meg heard the sound of ice cubes tinkling in glasses and her mother's soft laughter. Back in the living room they turned up the radio, and the dreamy sound of the Platters singing "The Great Pretender" came on.

Meg heard her mother say, "C'mon, Gus honey, les' dance."

"Shhh, quiet," Gus hissed. "Meg's asleep in the other room."

Her mind enveloped in alcohol, Irene whispered, "Never mind her, that kid sleeps like a log," and they started dancing.

In shock, Meg realized that her mother had come home with her father's best friend. Meg thought it was strange that they were still dancing after the music had stopped. They kept moving around the room, and they were real quiet, except for what sounded to her like sloppy kissing. No, it couldn't be. She strained her ears and listened harder.

Meg heard them again, laughing, giggling, talking soft and low, and then she heard other sounds...sounds of two people breathing very heavily, moaning noises...then the rhythmic squeaking of the springs on the old couch. With horror, Meg realized they were making love in the living room on the couch! She couldn't believe her mother could do something like this, or that she would do it right in her own living room. Irene wasn't always pleasant to her or to her dad, but this was something Meg had never dreamed her mother capable of.

Meg was so upset, she hid her head under the covers, put both hands over her mouth, and threw up in bed as quietly as she could. They probably wouldn't have heard her, anyway. She lay pitifully crying silently in the wet, sticky vomit until Gus had gone and her mother went to bed. Then Meg changed her sheets and alternately slept and cried the rest of the long, long night.

The next day she could scarcely bring herself to look her mother in the eyes. The sense of betrayal to both her and her father clenched in her stomach like a knot of snakes. She wondered if her dad knew about Irene. She wondered if this had happened before on those many other nights when Irene would leave and go home early from the Moose Club.

● ● ●

On Saturdays, the fantasy world of the Silver Screen was Meg's escape from the painful realities in her life. Every Saturday she'd walk all the way down Galena Avenue to the Patio Theater, quarter in hand, and see the movies playing that day. She'd stay and see them over and over again until it got dark. Sometimes her dad would have to come looking for her. At the movies she would pretend to be the elegant Audrey Hepburn in *Roman Holiday* or to have a lover like Cary Grant. She saw *Showboat* over and over again. In the movies, mothers were sweet and kind, and love was faithful and forever. She cried and sighed when Debra Paget died in Jeff Chandler's arms in *Broken Arrow*.

Surely every woman someday found that one love that could conquer anything. That kind of love had eluded Meg up to this point. She was already thirteen, but she had no prince of her own. He hadn't found her yet. Maybe, Meg reasoned, it was time she started actively looking for her life's love, a gentle love who would never leave her, never hurt her. She needed to feel someone's arms around her. She would have to be alert so she wouldn't miss him when he came along. Maybe she should start looking for him, not just wait for him to find her. He wouldn't be sorry.

Later that spring, Meg was confirmed in Saint Mary's Church in a beautiful ceremony. The ritual pageantry, solemn procession, colorful scented flowers, lacy white dresses, and beautiful music brought back conflicting memories of her First Communion six years ago. Those hideous recollections were all but forgotten, submerged and relegated to a safe place in her psyche, but they still left a painful and permanent scar on Meg's heart.

Saint Mary's Church and her religion were the backbone in her life, supplying Meg with a strong sense of belief and purpose. Within the Church, she found peace and acceptance. God loved her and cared about her, even if her mother didn't seem to.

5

Meg stood before the bathroom sink and primped, checking her reflection in the bathroom mirror. She applied a little bit of forbidden lipstick and touched up her eyebrows and eyelashes with a little Vaseline. Her long blonde ponytail was held in place with a printed chiffon scarf that matched her blue polished cotton full skirt, and two scatter pins shaped like cats, with rhinestones for eyes, adorned the round collar of her Peter Pan blouse. She cinched the wide black belt a notch tighter around her slim waist. Bending over, she rolled her thick socks just so, and with her hairbrush, roughed up the nap on her white bucks.

Satisfied with her look, she called out, "Gramps, I'm

going down to Roy's to meet Carol for a soda, okay? I won't be gone very long."

Her grandfather put down the *Life* magazine he had been reading in the living room and gave her a warm smile. "Okay, honey, if you have all your homework done. Just be sure you're back before your mother gets home from work. You know she doesn't like you out very long." He handed her a dollar. "Here's a little something for you to buy a soda, and would you mind picking up today's paper for me?"

She went over and gave him a hug. "Anything for you, Gramps, and thanks for the treat."

He looked up at her fondly. "You sure look pretty, Meg. You remind me of your grandma when she was young...."

Meg kissed him and then flew out the door of the apartment. At thirteen and a freshman in Catholic high school, Meg was starting to feel quite grown up. The gangly little kid had turned into a tall blonde beauty who was starting to fill out in all the right places and beginning to attract the attention of the opposite sex. She looked much older than her years, more like a girl of sixteen. Like her girlfriends, Meg had starting dating—just going to the movies, meeting boys at the soda shop, and sometimes studying together at their houses or hers. Sometimes they would go to a party at someone's house or meet at the city swimming pool. None of her friends were old enough to drive, so it was all pretty innocent and supervised.

Bouncing down the stairs, she was excited because she was meeting Denny. Roy's Soda Shop on Main Street was a popular neighborhood hangout after school, and all the kids gathered there to watch and flirt with each other, share gossip and dance to the jukebox. Most of the time, her mother wouldn't let her go, wanting her to stay at home and help with the housework, claiming it was a wild crowd that hung out there. Meg knew it was just the kids from her class, from her school, and nobody was wild. Irene just didn't like the idea that her little girl was growing up and was interested in having more freedom. Gramps was more lenient with her, remembering how it was to be young and full of the joy of life.

Denny, a boy who lived down the street from them in a beautiful wood and stone house, was someone she saw a lot of. They often walked to school together, sometimes went to the movies, and studied together. He was a nice boy and was good to her, important to a girl who wanted to be liked, loved, and noticed. Besides, he was fifteen, two years older than Meg, and was on the school football team, both of which put her up a notch in the eyes of her friends.

At the drugstore, she burst through the door into the room that was pounding with the sounds from the jukebox. There wasn't much in the way of a dance floor, but sometimes a couple just couldn't stand to sit still and would get up and dance. When they wanted to do some serious dancing, the kids would go to the Friday night dances at the JERK—the Junior Educational Recreational Center.

Waving to some of her friends as she came in the door, Meg caught a glimpse of Denny and slipped into the booth next to him. "Hi!" she said and cuddled close.

"Hey, babe, how ya doin'?" He nonchalantly put his arm around her in response to her pressure at his side as he scanned the crowd in the room. "You wanna Coke or something?" He went to the counter and soon returned with their drinks. The sounds of, "Shake, Rattle and Roll" filled the room with intense sound.

"Hey listen, Meg, I'm way behind in studying for that darned history test we're having tomorrow. You think you could help me with it? Maybe we could go over to your place and I could borrow your notes and you could quiz me a little." Meg was good in school, and this was one of the reasons Denny went out with her. Always eager to please, Meg was happy to help him out. After they finished their Cokes, they left, hand in hand.

Nobody was home when they got there. Her parents were both still at work, and her grandpa had left a note, saying he was going over to Fred Murphy's for a game of cards.

"You want some lemonade or an Orange Crush?" Meg offered. She went to get their drinks and turned the radio on softly. She liked to study with the music on. Like all teenagers of the fifties, she lived and breathed music. She and Denny settled in on the couch, papers and books spread out all over the coffee table. For nearly an hour, Meg quizzed him on the details of the Constitution and the colonies, her heart pounding at his closeness, unable to concentrate very well.

"Whew," Denny said, leaning back and stretching, "what do we need to know this dull history stuff for, anyway? I can't think of anything we'll ever use it for in the future." He turned to her and said, "Thanks again, Meggy, for helping me out." He really liked this kid. Her sunny disposition made her fun to be with, and she was sure helping him bring his grades up this year. Without her help, he probably would have been kicked off the football team because of his low grades.

Looking into her eyes, Denny suddenly saw a hunger beyond that of a girl her age. She had a soft, sensuous look that invited boys to be close to her. Something stirred in him, and he leaned over and gave her a kiss. What was meant to be a simple thank-you kiss, turned into something more. Closeness led to deeper kissing, and soon they were on her mother's bed, petting and excited beyond control. She wanted him to want her, and wanted to know what this thing called love was all about.

Their breathing heavy, both of them fumbled with their clothes, eager for forbidden contact. Denny kissed her neck and shoulders as he struggled with the hooks behind her back. They didn't even have all their clothes off before he eagerly entered her, thrusting strongly and quickly.

In shock, Meg thought, this hurts! It wasn't supposed

to be this way. What was all this talk about the magnificence and romance of love? To Meg, it was not very pleasant. If anything, it was painful, bringing back sad memories from long ago. She cried and sobbed afterwards. Meg didn't enjoy it at all, but Denny did. Most importantly, he held her close to him after it was all over, murmuring sweet things to her and telling her that he loved her, and that's all she had to hear. It made everything okay.

They started having sex on a fairly regular basis after that, maybe once a week or every couple of weeks, usually at her house, since nobody was at home after school. Gramps O'Conner had joined a card club, and two days a week he never got home until five. Meg didn't get much pleasure from the act itself, and she often felt guilty about it, but she craved the closeness, the holding, his murmured endearments afterward, and she felt she'd lose him if she said no.

Midterm finals were coming up, and Meg was helping Denny extra often with his math. He was pretty good in English, but couldn't seem to get the algebra. After having a turkey sandwich from the leftover Thanksgiving feast as a snack, they studied diligently. But now Denny had other things he wanted to study, and they weren't in schoolbooks.

"Denny," Meg protested, "I don't think we should. I've been kind of worried about this. What if I get pregnant?"

He brushed away her concerns. "Oh, you won't. It's the wrong time of the month, and I pull out every time so you won't get pregnant. Besides, you don't have to worry. If anything happened, I'd take care of it." He leaned over her and kissed her, pushing her back down on the couch.

They were so wrapped up in their passion, they didn't hear Meg's father unlock and come in the door. His malaria had flared up at work, exacerbated by the cold weather, and he'd had to leave work.

Meg sat up, startled. "Daddy! Wha…what are you doing home?" The look on his face made Meg feel ashamed.

All he said was, "Girlie, you get your clothes on. And you, buster, you better get out of here quick, and never let me see your face around here again."

Meg cried and got dressed, ashamed and fearful of what he would say or do. She knew what she'd done was wrong, but she just couldn't seem to help herself. She was embarrassed and felt guilty, and somehow she felt she'd let him down.

"Oh, Daddy, I'm so sorry. We were just studying and then we started kissing, and…."

Her father looked at her grimly and silently walked away. He didn't hit her or call her names or give her a lecture, he just walked away. His heart was broken inside, but he knew Meg wasn't a bad girl at heart. She was just too loving, too naive. He never mentioned that incident to Irene, never.

Denny didn't call again, but she soon discovered that she had gained a reputation. Most of the nice boys didn't seem to want anything to do with her, and a lot of the girls at school giggled and whispered behind her back whenever she passed them by in the halls. She felt dirty, humiliated, and ashamed, as if everybody knew.

• • •

She'd met Larry while she was walking to school one day. He lived just a few blocks down the street from her and had been out tinkering on his car early one morning. She'd stopped to admire his custom hot rod and they'd struck up a conversation.

"Pretty hot car you have there," she remarked. "Are those glasspack mufflers?"

He was impressed with her knowledge of cars. "Yeah. Cost me a pretty penny, too. Had to work extra weekends at the Amoco station. You live around here?"

She pointed to her apartment building. "I'm on the way to school, Aquin High. Well, I gotta go. 'Bye."

"Wait a minute, what's your name?"

"Meg...Meg O'Conner. What's yours?"

"Larry Blake." She started to walk away and he called, "Why don't you stop by again on your way to school tomorrow, okay?"

There was nothing romantic between them at first. They were just pals, talking about cars and music, and he'd buy cigarettes for her. Once in a while in the morning she'd go to his house before school, after his mother left for work, and they'd drink Mogan David sweet red wine. On those days she could barely stagger to school, but drinking made her feel good and dulled her senses to where she didn't have to think about the things she'd seen and done, the things that had happened to her that hurt so much inside, and the things she was so ashamed of and yet couldn't quit doing. She didn't especially like the drinking, as later it usually made her feel sick. At school, she'd bump into lockers and fall asleep in class, sometimes even getting sick enough to throw up. Her excuse was that she must have the flu; she had the flu a lot that year.

Before long, she and Larry started dating and soon became lovers. He was tall and attractive, with a wanton sort of wild look she found exciting, sort of like Marlon Brando. For Meg, her love for Larry became love for life. She needed somebody to care about her, somebody to hold her and make her feel wanted, and he seemed to fill that need. He accepted her and wanted her. They'd go to his house after school and make love as often as they could. He was a much better lover than Denny, and she just knew this was her true love forever. They got engaged, without her parents knowing it. He was seventeen, she was thirteen.

In her search for identity and acceptance, Meg started running around with Larry's friends, an older, different type of crowd—guys who wore black leather jackets and black boots, all riding big motorcycles. They smoked and drank and had tattoos, and most of them boxed in the Golden Gloves. They used to hang out at Elm's Pool Hall, their bikes parked in a row out in front.

• • •

"Hey, Larry, got a light?" she asked, sliding onto the stool at the bar. She held up her Winston to receive the flame as he clicked open his Zippo lighter. She was waiting her turn to play a game of rotation pool.

Meg brushed an ash off of her tight black skirt and tugged her mohair sweater down around her hips. She'd started wearing tight sweaters and tight skirts and nylons, and as soon as she was out the door of their apartment, she'd apply more make-up. She felt very grown up, tough and sexy, building a shell around herself to hide the vulnerable need for acceptance inside. She started drinking and smoking with the crowd, hiding her cigarettes in her old doll buggy at home.

She was so very much in love with Larry, and she knew he had to love her, too, although he'd never said it out loud. Uncle Sam, however, had other plans. Larry was drafted and sent to Fort Leonardwood, Missouri. Oh, how she missed him! She wrote to him every day, sending him pictures, pieces of her hair, and once in a while she'd borrow Cindy's tape recorder and record long, sultry conversations about what she was doing, what was happening in town, and how much she missed him. She ached to see him, hear his voice, touch his hair.

Her friend Cindy, who she'd known since fourth grade, was the only one of her old friends who still stuck by her. She loved Meg and knew she was going through a very confusing time in her life. She didn't like Larry at all and she thought he was too old for Meg, too wild, and she didn't trust him.

At Cindy's house one Saturday afternoon in March before they left to go to the movies, Cindy tried to talk some sense in her. "Meg, why don't you come over after the movie? We'll make some popcorn, and I have the newest issue of *Star and Screen*."

It sounded like fun to Meg, but she wanted to get back home in case Larry called. "Thanks, Cindy, but I gotta get home. Larry said he might call tonight."

"I think you're making a big mistake, moping around and waiting for that guy to call. He's too old for you, and I think you're wasting your time, Meg. I know you've been true blue to that creep, but I heard Larry's been going out with other girls while he's been stationed down there."

"Who told you that?" Meg asked angrily, standing up from Cindy's bed.

"Gee, everybody knows about it. Freeport isn't that big a town, you know. If you must know, it was his sister, Jackie. One night at Roy's I overheard her talking about this new girl he was going out with down in Missouri."

Meg felt betrayed. She knew she'd never cheat on Larry. They were engaged. Oh, she didn't have a ring or anything, but he had asked her to wait for him. How could he? Her heart was broken, and she felt abandoned again.

While Larry was gone, she spent a lot of time with Jackie, his sister. Like Meg, Jackie loved to go to the movies, and they saw a lot of them. Jackie slightly resembled Grace Kelly, and their favorite movie for a while was *The Country Girl*.

One Friday evening, Jackie and Meg had been to the movies, and after they came back to her house, Jackie left to see her boyfriend. Meg didn't want to go home so soon. She tried not to spend too much time at home. Whenever she was home, she always seemed to get into arguments with her mother about something, and it was safer to be gone. Besides, the Blakes had a television set, and Meg could sit and watch Jackie Gleason and Ed Sullivan for hours.

Jackie's mom asked her if she wanted to stay and brought her a glass of iced tea. Larry's older brother, Ray, was there, too, and after the TV show was over, they decided to play a game of gin rummy.

"So, how did you like the movie?" he asked as he dealt out the cards.

"Oh, I love the movies!" she said exuberantly. "I practically live there. Tonight we saw that new movie, *The Wild Ones*. Marlon Brando has the sexiest eyes."

Ray shot a glance at Meg, and decided to take a chance. He knew his little brother wasn't interested in Meg any longer. "Nothing compared to yours, Meg. You're the prettiest girl I've seen in this town. Larry is stupid, not appreciating a gorgeous girl like you." He reached across the card table and touched her hand.

Meg's heart jumped into her throat. Ray was much older, nineteen, sexy, and was really built. She never thought he even noticed her.

"Hey, you wanna take a spin on my Harley? It's a beautiful night, and we could go out to Krape Park."

Meg had never actually ridden on one of the big, powerful bikes, and with the magical memory of the movie in her mind, she agreed. On the back of the powerful machine, she felt like she was part of the *Wild Ones*, the wind in her hair, her arms around this strong young man, her cheek pressed against his black motorcycle jacket, inhaling the smell of supple leather.

At the park he put down a soft blanket and produced a couple of beers from the bike's saddlebags. He put his arm around her cardigan-clad shoulders and pulled her to him in a long, lingering kiss. What was happening here? This was Larry's brother! Then she remembered how Larry had cheated on her, and in her anger thought, why not? I can cheat as much as he did. This would be the ultimate betrayal.

The following weekend, Ray invited her to a Golden Gloves match in Rockford. Her parents reluctantly let her go, since his family was going to attend the match, but Meg's father disliked Ray, saying he was too old for her, and he disapproved of his wild biker ways and friends.

That night when Ray brought her home, they were

necking out in the front hall, nothing heavy, just necking. Meg leaned against the wall next to their apartment door and Larry bent over to kiss her lingeringly, his hand behind her head, fingers lost in the golden threads of her silky hair.

Suddenly, Meg's father came flying out the front door. He must have been drinking, because Meg had never seen him act like this before. Enraged, he grabbed Ray's shirt and pulled him within inches of his face.

"Listen, punk, I know about you and your wild biker friends, and I know you've been taking Meg over to that sleazy pool hall without our permission. Here's a little something I'll bet you didn't know. Meg is only thirteen years old, and you could be prosecuted for statutory rape if you don't keep your hands off her!"

He gave Ray a shove and managed to send him tumbling down a whole flight of stairs. He wasn't hurt, but got the message. Ray saw no future in pursuing a thirteen-year-old girl, no matter how beautiful she was or how well built.

The story of her father's rage got around, and Meg's social life cooled off for a while after that. In a way, she was glad. She was tired of pretending to be sophisticated and older than she was. And she missed Cindy and Debbie and her old friends.

• • •

In the midst of these tumultuous changes in her life, while she was trying to discover a way to grow up, her dearest and best friend, Grandpa O'Conner, died. When he died, a part of Meg died, too. She felt like a piece of her heart, a piece of her life, had been cut out of her, and she was bleeding but nobody could see. She cried for days, bereft and alone. She was lost without him and felt numb with pain until the day of the funeral.

When she went forward at the mortuary to view the body, the reality of it all knifed through her. When she saw him resting so still and quiet in that pale blue satin and metal oblong box, she realized he was really going to leave her forever. "Oh, Gramps, please come back. Please don't leave me. I won't have anybody to talk to now. Oh, please, how could you leave me?" she wailed.

She ran to him, threw her arms around her beloved Gramps, and hugged him tight, praying that somehow she might bring him back to her. They had to forcibly drag her away.

The funeral was a blur of pain and tears. Her one thought was that she couldn't bear to have him buried alone because he would miss her. Taking some manicure scissors out of her purse, she cut off a large hank of her long, gorgeous hair and placed it in her grandfather's hands before they closed the casket. She knew then that she would always be with him, and in some way they would always be together, no matter what.

First it was Sister Augustus, and now her cherished Gramps. It seemed like everyone she ever loved or trusted always hurt her or abandoned her.

6

By 1956, Roy's Soda Shop had become fifteen-year-old Meg's second home. After her breakup with Ray, she'd drifted away from the rough, hard motorcycle crowd. Life was too much fun to hang around with such tough characters. Besides, most of her girlfriends liked to hang around at Roy's, flirting with boys, listening to records on the jukebox, and dancing.

"Hey, Trish!" Cindy called to Meg as she poked her head into the door of Roy's. (They always used their nicknames, Trish and Kitty, these days.) "Are you going over to the JERK tonight, or are you and Chuck going to the Halloween party out at the park? Everybody's going! You should see my costume. I'm gonna be one of the good witches, like from *The Wizard of Oz*. There's gonna be a band, maybe even The Lords from Rockford, and Eddie's getting some beer. Come with me over to Woolworth's. I need to get some hair spray and some nail polish, and that new record by Elvis Presley is out, too."

Meg smiled. How Cindy could say all that in one breath was beyond her, but that was one of the things she liked about her—her exuberance. "Maybe later," Meg said with a smile. "I'm waiting for Chuck. He's meeting me here pretty soon, and we might go work on his car for a little while."

She'd met Chuck Wagner right there at Roy's one day as she was leafing through the magazine and comic book rack. He'd reached for the same movie magazine, and their eyes had met. Something electric happened, and after they'd shared a soda, he had asked her to go to the movies that Friday night.

She'd been going out with another guy, Bobby Ross, at the time and Chuck was just sort of hanging around, a part of their gang, but she didn't really know him very well. She never thought he'd ask her out for a date because he came from an entirely different class of people than she did. She was the girl from the wrong side of the tracks, a poor girl from a poor family. Chuck came from a well-to-do family that had everything. His father was a doctor and they even belonged to the country club out on the edge of town.

Chuck was a tall, good-looking guy who resembled Sal Mineo, with dark, curly hair and dark eyes. He had kind of an innocent, waif-like look about him that she found endearing. She'd really flipped for him, and she guessed he'd fallen for her, too. They had become an "item," dating only each other, and had been going out exclusively for about three months now.

She swiveled around on the red Naugahyde seat at the counter and moved to put some money in the flashing Wurlitzer jukebox. After reading down the columns, she punched the numbers of some of her favorite songs—"Come Go With Me," by the Dell-Vikings, and "Searchin'" by the Coasters. If she'd had more change, she would have picked a few numbers by Elvis, her newest favorite. At fifteen, Meg was beautiful and popular, a cheerleader on the junior varsity squad at Aquin Catholic High School, and doing well in school.

She and her best friends, Cindy and Debby, belonged to a car club of about two dozen kids called "The Rebels," and always wore their black satin jackets with a rebel flag stitched on the back, their names embroidered in flourishing script on the front over their hearts. It wasn't the type of gang that caused trouble or did anything illegal, it was just a way of signifying who they were and that they were all together. Each of them knew if there ever was any kind of trouble, all they had to do was call on everybody else. On weekends caravans of cars with all the Rebels in them cruised up and down Main Street in Freeport between the A&W Root Beer at one end of town and the Dairy Queen at the other. In the summers, they'd all go to the Galaxy Drive-In and park together, running back and forth between cars, visiting and horsing around.

The guys in the club spent most of their time fixing up their old jalopies—chopping and channeling them, getting just the right metallic paint job, customizing the paint jobs with pin stripes, and making their cars extensions of their personalities. None of the girls had cars, but they went out with boys who did. All of them had nicknames to make them feel even more a part of the club.

Chuck had a hot '52 Ford that he'd painted a slick candy-apple red. It had spun chrome baby moon hubcaps, and the thing was set on a twenty-degree rake to make it look even jazzier. The interior was done in black tuck and roll, with fuzzy white dice hanging from the rearview mirror.

They painted the dashboard a shiny jet black, and Meg handpainted little white spiderwebs all over it. In the back window she took black and white material and sewed it together to resemble a checkerboard pattern.

On the outside, Chuck had taken off all the chrome strips, hood ornaments, the trunk decal and the door handles and had installed electronic gadgets so that all they had to do was press on the side of the door and it would open. It had dual glass-packs with chrome extensions and a souped-up engine that made it rumble like a caged lion.

She'd helped him do some pin-striping and detailing on the windows, and they had a sign that said "The Rebels" displayed in the back window. Meg was happy with her contribution to the way his car looked. She felt proud to be seen with him when they went to the pep rallies and football games and out to the parties in the park on Friday nights. It was probably the best time in her life. Sex was a big part of that fun, too, and she and Chuck really had a thing going. For the first time in her life, Meg was enjoying it, too. Chuck really seemed to love her, and this time she was sure it was forever.

As she turned from the jukebox, she saw Chuck walking in and hurried over to slip her arm through his. "Hi, Chuck," she said brightly, looking up at him with a smile.

"Hi, Meg. Hey, this is a great tune, doll, you wanna dance?" He whirled her out onto the tiny floor to the tune of "Party Doll." He was a great dancer and she was, too, and soon they had quite an audience watching them on the small dance floor. Her blonde hair flew and her lavender full skirt whirled as he spun her around. The number over, they tumbled into a booth and ordered Cherry Cokes and fries.

"Chuck, Eddie and the gang are all going out to the park tonight for the Halloween party. Are we still going? If we are, I have to get home pretty soon to finish up our costumes." Chuck was going to go as Yul Brynner in *The King and I*, and Meg was planning to dress up like a harem girl to complement his costume. She'd even taken one of her mother's old swim caps and painted it to look like skin so Chuck would look like he had a bald head.

"Do you still want to go, or do you just want to work on

the Roadrunner some more tonight?" She wanted to go to the party, but she would do anything he wanted to please him.

Chuck thought for a minute, then replied, "I guess since you've put so much work into the costumes, we might as well go." He wasn't much for parties, but he liked hanging out with the gang. "I guess I can pick up that special paint tomorrow and we can work on the car then. The party sounds like fun, and I heard that The Lords will be playing out there tonight. It'll be a nice change." He gave her arm a squeeze as they got up to go.

At the park, the Rebels would position their cars in a circle and turn on the headlights, creating an impromptu dance floor. With all the radios tuned to the same station, the kids would dance in the circle of light, fast and slow, to tunes like "Rock Around the Clock," "Whispering Bells," and "There Goes My Baby." Some of the guys were old enough to buy beer, and there was always a steady supply. And, of course, there was always the friendly darkness outside the circle of headlights where a couple could find a quiet spot for a more romantic, private sort of dance.

Meg came home and tiptoed quietly into her mother's room to get the sewing kit. As usual, her mother was in bed, probably zonked out on prescription pain killers. Meg still did most of the housework, cooking, and taking care of her father.

At the fabric store sale last week, they'd had a clearance on all fabrics, and Meg managed to get enough material to make a vest of fancy brocade for Chuck and the harem costume for herself. She'd found a bunch of chiffon scarves at the second-hand store and added those to the costume for veils.

She worked on Saturdays as a bus girl at Capone's, a fancy Italian restaurant near where Chuck lived, and she'd spent nearly all of her tip money to make the costumes for herself and Chuck. And if she had to say so herself, they looked pretty terrific.

Chuck picked her up early for the party so they could go by and pick up Cindy and her date. The weather was a warm and balmy Indian summer night, and Meg's body glowed with the pleasure of youth. It felt like the warm night air was stroking her skin, making her feel alive and beautiful.

It was a magical evening. Her friends had turned into enchanted creatures and wondrous beings for the night, and she and Chuck were the envy of her girlfriends, with their matching costumes. They danced, drank a little beer, and made sweet love on a soft blanket on a bed of leaves.

When he brought her home at midnight, they kissed good night on the apartment porch. "See you at school on Monday," Chuck called as he bounded down the stairs to his car.

Life didn't get much better than this, Meg thought to herself as she heard his car rumble off. She had a sweet guy who had a great car. She had super friends, was doing pretty well in school and was a popular cheerleader. She hugged her arms around herself in sheer happiness and stepped dreamily up the stairs to their apartment.

As she quietly closed the door behind herself, she saw her mother sitting in the shadows on the big, overstuffed chair. She had a glass and a half-empty bottle of bourbon next to her.

"Hi, Mom," Meg said happily, and went over to kiss her good night. "Oh, you should have seen the costumes at the party. It was so much...."

"Where have you been to all hours of the night, you slut?" her mother yelled, pushing herself unsteadily up out of the red mohair chair. "You've been drinking, haven' you?" She made her way through the dim living room with her arm raised to strike Meg.

"Remember, Mom...the Halloween party? I went with Chuck...You said I could go," she pleaded, backing away with her arms raised protectively before her.

Irene beat with her fists against Meg's upraised arms.

"Jus' look at tha' sleazy costume. You oughta be 'shamed. Get in your room right now!"

Meg turned and fled to her room, hoping her mother wouldn't follow, but she was not so lucky. Irene flung open the door and knocked Meg down on her bed. "I'll teach you how to behave, you li'l whore!" She began to punch Meg ruthlessly. Meg curled up into a defensive ball. She couldn't hit her mother back, as that would make her even madder.

Suddenly, the blows stopped. "Irene! Leave her alone and get back to bed!" It was her father, and he had ahold of her mother's wrists, pushing her backward out of her bedroom. "You've been drinking, and you don't know what you're doing. Just leave the girl alone," he said again firmly but softly.

She glared hatefully at him but turned away, muttering as she staggered down the hall, "Bitch. Jus' makes my life mizzable...."

Her father gently closed the door behind him as Meg buried her face in her pillow, sobbing.

● ● ●

Meg was really excited about going to the Christmas dance at school. It would be her first formal dance. Chuck had asked her to go last week, and she was in a whirl. Her mother would never buy her a dress, so she was borrowing one of Cindy's gowns that didn't fit her any longer.

At Cindy's house, the two girls had been trying out new hairstyles, primping and getting ready. They'd spent the afternoon in curlers, painting their fingernails and toenails, giggling and gossiping. The Emerson radio was playing hit tunes in the background.

"This dress will look better on you, anyway," Cindy told her as Meg stood before her friend's bedroom mirror holding the gown up to her. "That soft pink goes great with your gorgeous eyes. I wish I had green eyes, or maybe lavender eyes like Elizabeth Taylor." Cindy paused, and then, changing the subject, said wistfully, "You and Chuck have been going out for about four months now, haven't you, Trish?" They always used their Rebel club nicknames.

Meg smiled and replied, "I'm sure this is the real thing. I really love him, Kitty. And I think he loves me."

"Gee, I wish I could find somebody steady. Tony's taking me to the dance, but he's kind of a drip. Nobody wants to treat me romantic. They all treat me like some kind of a pal, or a big sister. I guess they all think I'm too fat or something," her friend complained, sucking on a Coca-cola and munching on a handful of potato chips.

Meg was quick to come to her friend's defense. "Oh no, maybe you just need a little more make-up, something to highlight your great bone structure. Here, let's try a few things." Meg was always good at fixing hair and doing make-up and wanted to help her friend. "See? It makes a big difference if you just use some dark blue eye shadow there and line your eyes with some black eyeliner. And see," she said, grabbing her friend's chestnut hair, "if you piled your hair on top of your head tonight, it would make your face seem slimmer, more exotic."

The girls giggled and continued to gossip about who was going with whom to the dance, what to wear, how to fix their hair, and other girl talk. Their dates would be there soon to pick them up.

When the doorbell rang, Cindy's parents answered the door so the girls could make their grand entrance. Meg's eyes lit up when she saw her date. Chuck was wearing a white sport coat and carried a florist box in his hand. When his eyes saw Meg, they opened wide in appreciation.

"Wow, you look gorgeous! I'll be the envy of every guy there tonight."

Meg blushed at the compliment and took the box he proffered. Inside, instead of the usual wrist or dress corsage, was an enormous fragrant white gardenia, devised to be pinned in her upswept hair.

That night, Chuck gave her his class ring and asked her officially to be his girl. Meg was surprised, because she knew his parents didn't particularly approve of her. They were real muckity-mucks, and Chuck's mom even used to follow him sometimes in her car to make sure he wasn't going to see that little tramp, Meg.

"Oh, Chuck," she said softly, "I love you so much!"

In the romantic darkness of the school auditorium, he took her in his arms and whispered in her ear, "I want everyone to know that you're my girl." They later made love in the back seat of the Ford.

• • •

She was sixteen and she was pregnant and what was she going to do now? Her mother always told her she was a slut and a whore. She didn't feel like one, but people kept talking about her like she was, including her own mother. She was scared to death to tell her parents. Nice Catholic girls didn't get themselves in this predicament. Chuck's parents were so class-conscious, she could just imagine what they would say.

Panic set in. Meg was frantic. Trying to figure out a solution, one afternoon after school she sat in Roy's Soda Shop. Staring into her root beer float, suddenly she started to cry. Cindy, ever her best friend, hurried over to see what the matter was. Eddie, a good-looking guy in the Rebels who had always liked Meg, also came up and wanted to know what was wrong. Before she could stop herself, Meg blurted out everything.

"I'm pregnant, and I don't know what to do," she sobbed. "I can't tell my mom, she'd kill me. And if I tell my dad, it'll just break his heart. It's Chuck's, you know that, but his parents don't think I'm good enough for him, and he's supposed to go to college, and...."

"Hey, no problem. The best thing to do is to run away," Eddie suggested. "That way nobody will find out what's going on. At least it'll buy you some time to think."

It sounded outrageous, but in her panic, it seemed like a good solution. At least she wouldn't have to face her mother right away. Eddie, Meg and Cindy scraped together all the money they could between them, threw a few things into Meg's mother's Samsonite, and jumped on a train to Cincinnati.

The first few nights there they stayed in a dingy fleabag hotel, all three of them sleeping in the same bed. Nothing sexual went on. They were just three buddies trying to work out a very serious problem. But after a few days, their money ran out, they had to leave the hotel, and they were hungry. They ended up sleeping in the railroad station, cold and hungry and begging for money to buy food.

One night Meg was approached by a man who looked kind and as if he could afford a few quarters. Meg was the best at panhandling…something about her innocent, sweet looks made people want to help her out. Unfortunately, the nice-looking man turned out to be a railroad detective. He and his men had been watching the three teenagers as they hung around and talked to a lot of people. Somehow they had the mistaken notion that they were selling drugs.

When Meg and Cindy went into the rest room, three cops came in the door, pulled guns on them, and put them under arrest. When they came out of the rest room, every exit of the railroad station was covered by a uniformed officer. The three were arrested and taken to jail.

They were separated and taken to juvenile hall, where Meg spent two frightening nights in jail. The authorities didn't believe they were just panhandling, but had no evidence upon which to convict them. The police finally called their parents, and Meg's dad wired some money to send her back home on the train. The warden's bodyguard, named Ezzard Charles, an ex-championship boxer, escorted Meg to the train and put her on it. It was the longest train ride of her life. She rode home with a knot in her stomach, knowing what she'd have to face when she got home.

The inquisition began. "Young lady, you have a lot of explaining to do," her mother yelled at her. "Your father and I were worried sick about you. Why did you run away? And where did you get the money? You stole it out of my purse, didn't you? Your father and I work hard for every penny we get, not to have you steal it and go gallivanting around the country like some gypsy! Where did you go? Who were you with? Some of your no-good motorcycle bum friends, I'll bet."

Meg looked at the floor and cringed inside. She had to tell them, but didn't know how she was going to do it. She took a deep breath and swallowed hard. Looking at her feet, she said softly, "Mother, I'm pregnant. I ran away because I was scared and didn't know what else to do." Tears were flowing down her cheek.

When her mother heard that news, she flew into a rage. "Pregnant! You God-damned slut! Now you'll never get that decent Chuck Wagner to marry you. I knew something like this would happen with you sleeping around with every boy in town!" She grabbed Meg's arm in a vice-like grip and slapped her hard. Her hand was raised to strike the other cheek, but Meg's father stepped in.

"Just a minute, Irene. That isn't going to solve anything. We have to think about what to do now, and hitting her won't solve anything." He looked at Meg with great sadness in his eyes, then put his comforting arms around her sobbing shoulders.

In Cincinnati, the three had already decided that she would say the baby was Eddie's and not Chuck's, since marrying Chuck seemed like such a hopeless situation. He was someone a girl like Meg could never have. She was the girl from the wrong side of the tracks—fun to be with at parties, fun to fool around with, but not the kind of girl somebody like Chuck would or could marry. Since it seemed there was no future for her and Chuck, when Eddie suggested they say the baby was his, it seemed reasonable to Meg. It might work.

"It's Eddie Decker's baby. He said he'd marry me," she said quietly.

No one questioned how or when, which Meg thought was strange, considering she had dated Chuck for nearly six months, and she had never once dated Eddie.

•••

In late February of 1958, Eddie Decker and Meg O'Conner were married by a justice of the peace in a small ceremony. It seemed like the only thing to do. At least it absolved her mother of the problem of figuring out what to do about the situation. She wouldn't have to explain about her pregnant unwed daughter to her card club friends. Meg was just sixteen.

Eddie and Meg were living in Meg's room in her parents' apartment. Eddie still hadn't found a job. He didn't even seem to be looking for one very hard. He spent most of his time hanging out with his buddies and working on cars.

Meg wanted to be able to afford an apartment and move out of there, away from her parents, and soon. She didn't want to nag him, but he didn't seem to be making much of an effort.

"Eddie, have you looked at the morning paper today?" she asked, holding the want ads in her hand. "I glanced through it after breakfast, and it looks like there's a couple of jobs that might work out for you. There's one down at the Sinclair gas station that might be good. You could work on cars and…."

"Hey, quit buggin' me," he yelled at her, slapping the newspaper out of her hand. "I told ya I'll get a damn job, but I'll be the one to do it, and when I'm damned good and ready, so just get off my back!" He shoved her so hard she fell back against the kitchen table and nearly fell.

"I'm sorry, I was just trying to help," Meg replied, rubbing the backs of her legs where they'd crashed into the table.

"Well, don't!" he yelled and slammed out of the apartment.

Right after they were married sweet, concerned, caring, loving Eddie began to change into another person. Some innate hatred and anger surfaced inside of him, and he started to push and shove Meg around for real or imagined transgressions. Their lovemaking, which had been sweet in the beginning, couldn't even be called sex these days. It was brutal, almost like rape, with little participation on her part.

That night when he came home for dinner, he seemed even more tense than usual. He slammed into their bedroom right after he'd finished eating. Meg did the dishes and followed, wanting to talk to him about what was wrong.

He attacked her verbally right away. "You think you're so damned high and mighty, don't you? Trying to tell me what to do. Well, where the hell would you be right now if it wasn't for me? Huh? You'd be having a bastard kid with no father. And what do I get out of the deal? Nothin' but complaints." He was pacing back and forth in the small room, banging his fists against his jean-clad thighs.

Meg was used to listening to his tirades and knew most of the time to just let him ramble on and get it all out. She started folding some clothes that were on the dresser while he spouted off.

"Don't you turn your back on me, woman." He grabbed her shoulder and spun her around to face him. Meg was frightened. She'd never seen him act this violently. He'd slapped and pushed her before, but never had she seen this crazy look in his eyes.

"Eddie, calm down. What's wrong?" she said, and reached out to try to calm him down.

Slapping her hand down, he yelled, "You're what's wrong, bitch!" He hurled her toward the bed, and as she stumbled, he kicked her in the back with his motorcycle boot. The fact that she was pregnant didn't seem to matter.

Hysterical, she ran from the room into the arms of her father. Meg knew she had to get out of this mess, and this time her parents backed her up and decided to help.

Their marriage was annulled in April of 1958. Meg had to lie in court about the circumstances of him marrying her so they could get the annulment, but that was better than a lengthy divorce. The most important thing was to get out of this terrible situation.

When Chuck found out she'd had the marriage annulled, he began calling and coming over to see her. He started asking a lot of pointed questions about the baby, because he just couldn't believe it was Eddie's. He knew Meg had been faithful to him all the while they had been dating, and he knew Eddie wasn't the type of guy Meg would go out with, anyway. She wanted to tell him the truth.

That May of 1958 was a sad time for her. In the soft spring night, she sat on the front porch of their apartment house and watched Chuck drive by in his car with his date for the Senior Prom. She held her growing belly and rubbed it and cried, longing for her carefree teenage days.

7

That July, Meg finally told Chuck the truth about the baby. He'd been asking questions and dropping hints, as though he'd known all along.

They were sitting on the front porch after going to see *The Bridge on the River Kwai*, enjoying the evening coolness, watching the fireflies and drinking iced tea, and Meg just blurted it out. "Uh...Chuck, maybe you should know. This isn't Eddie's baby. It's yours. You're the only one I was with that whole time." She wasn't sure what she wanted from him...marriage, financial support, or just for him to know it was his. But she couldn't keep the truth from him any longer.

Chuck half turned to her in the twilight. "I knew it all

along, Meg. You never even dated that creep, Eddie." He reached out and took her hand and they sat in silence as the twilight deepened into night.

Chuck didn't know what to do. He had college plans and wasn't sure he was ready for this kind of responsibility. He knew his parents didn't approve of Meg, but he also knew they'd like her if they'd just give her a chance. He loved Meg, but he couldn't figure out what to do about this. He'd started seeing Meg again, but no plans were made as Meg's belly continued to grow.

She was out with Chuck at the movies when her water broke and she went into labor. Nobody had ever filled her in on the facts of childbearing, and she was terrified when the pains began. It was one week past her seventeenth birthday.

"Oh God, Chuck, this hurts!" She was standing in the lobby of the movie theater, holding her belly and squinting her eyes up tight with the pain.

He hovered around her helplessly, not knowing what to do, either. Should he call the manager? Should he take her to the hospital? He decided he'd better call Irene, but there was no one home.

"Meg, where are your parents tonight? Nobody's home, nobody's answering the telephone. Think. Where are they right now?"

"Uh, I think they're at the bowling alley. Tonight's a regular league game. Call there and see," she urged, gasping at the onslaught of another strong contraction. More than anything, she wanted to get out of the lobby of the theater. Her dress was wet, and she didn't think she could stand up by herself much longer.

Chuck finally reached them at the bowling alley. "Irene, Meg's having the baby, right now! What? Okay, here she is." He handed the phone to Meg.

"Mother, I think I'm having the baby," she cried over the phone. "What do I do now?"

Irene was excited about the baby, but perturbed because her bowling game had been interrupted. "Just get back home, Meg, and I'll be right there."

Irene came home, quickly packed a suitcase for Meg, and they hurried to the hospital. Meg was so small the nurses couldn't believe she was full term and in labor, but they finally admitted her and began getting her ready for the process of giving birth. First came the horrible enema and the shave. She felt degraded and defiled.

She remembered clinging to the bars on the headboard at the back of the bed, screaming her lungs out. There were no pain killers to ease the agony of that long labor. Nobody had told her anything about what to expect. Finally, just when she thought she couldn't stand another minute of the ordeal, she cried out to her mother.

"Mama, I think my guts are coming out!"

Irene looked and could see the baby's head protruding. She immediately called a nurse and then proceeded to slide down the woodwork of the doorway in a dead faint.

There was no doctor there! The nurses tried to hold Meg's legs together to delay the birth, but then rushed her into a delivery room and an intern slipped a gas mask on her face. On September 20, 1958 at 4:45 A.M. her son was born, and she didn't remember a thing about it.

When her mother came into her room later to visit, Meg strained to sit up. She felt sore and tired all over. "Oh, Mama, did you see him? Isn't little Matt an angel?" They talked for a little while, and then Meg added, "I'm glad he's here, but I didn't know having a baby was going to be so much work and hurt so much."

Irene snorted and replied, "You think you had a hard time? I was in labor for two days with you, and they had to pull you out with forceps. I thought I was going to die. There was never so much pain in the world. Besides that, I got as big as a house and had ankles the size of watermelons." And with that, she got up and left. Meg sat in silence for a long time and wondered how Irene would respond to Matt. Would she, could she, love him?

It's a funny thing about becoming a mother. When they place that precious miracle in your arms, you forget about any discomfort and all the pain. As Meg cuddled her newborn son close to her heart, she said out loud, "At last I have someone who will always be mine and who no one can ever take away from me." Those words would come back to haunt Meg a few years later. She loved her new little son so much she thought her heart would burst.

Chuck came to see her and the baby while they were in the hospital. He brought her a bouquet of flowers, and for Matt he brought a football bigger that little Matt himself. Little Matthew was tiny—he weighed only 4 pounds 14 ounces—and they wouldn't let him come home from the hospital when Meg was released; he had to stay until he weighed five and a half pounds.

It was heartbreaking for Meg to go home with empty arms, without her baby. She spent a lot of time at the hospital, looking at Matt through the nursery window. Sometimes the nurses would let her hold him, with his fragile hand wrapped around her index finger, her breath stirring the downy-soft hair on top of his head. Finally, after about ten days, the doctors judged he was big enough and strong enough to come home with her. Meg was ecstatic.

She had fixed up one corner of her room with a little bassinet and moved some of her clothes to a box in the closet so she could put his layette things in her dresser. She had a little enameled white basin that she used to give him a bath, and fixed the top of her dresser as a changing table. She never wanted him to be very far out of her sight.

He was so little, however, that they couldn't circumcise him immediately, and so she had to endure bringing him back to the hospital when he was two months old for that dreadful procedure. Oh, how it hurt her to give them her baby, knowing he was going to suffer.

Of course, Irene took over when Matt came home after the procedure, as if it were her baby instead of Meg's.

"Meg, you shouldn't put so much Karo syrup in that baby's formula, it'll give him cramps. And how long did you boil those bottles before you took them out of the sterilizer? I swear, you have to be told how to do everything." No matter what she tried to do, her mother made it clear she was doing it wrong and that only she knew what was best for the baby. Meg couldn't diaper, feed, or hold the baby right. She couldn't do anything right.

Chuck's mother still hadn't accepted the baby as being Chuck's, even though Chuck had told her about little Matt and spent most of his spare time over at Meg's with her and the baby.

One day, fed up with the situation, Meg dressed little Matt up in his very best, marched over to the Wagner house and rang the doorbell.

When Chuck's mother opened the door, Meg announced, "This is your grandson," and handed him to her. She either had to hold him or drop him on the ground. It took only one look for her to fully realize and admit this was Chuck's son. As little as Matt was, he looked exactly like Chuck—the same small face, dimple in his chin, and curly, dark hair. And whether she liked it or not, Meg and Chuck were making plans to be married in his church that spring. As much as Chuck's mother disliked her and couldn't stand the idea of his being married to a "girl like her," she had no choice but to accept it now.

• • •

When Matt was six months old, on March 19, 1959, Chuck and Meg were married. Meg felt at long last they could truly be a family. That's all she'd ever really wanted, someone to love her, a family and babies of her own. They found their own little apartment, and Chuck even made arrangements to have Matt's name legally changed from O'Conner to Wagner to protect him in later years. Since he had been born six months before they were married, Meg's maiden name was on the birth certificate.

Without much money, they left Matt with Meg's parents for a couple of days and honeymooned in their little apartment. On their honeymoon night Meg wanted to be real sexy for him. This was the beginning of a new life for both of them, so special and rare.

After they'd had a few drinks, she lit a bunch of candles and slipped on a filmy, sexy, short nightgown she had bought especially for this night. The theme from the movie *The Apartment* was playing softly on the radio, and Chuck was standing expectantly beside the bed. She slithered seductively across the room, doing a sort of strip tease for him, trying to act as grown up as she could at seventeen.

Suddenly he burst out laughing. When she'd whisked off the nightie at the end of her sexy dance, it had floated down to land on the end of his hardened member! They laughed so hard they couldn't breathe. It took awhile to become composed enough to make love, but it was a great start to the marriage.

Secretly, in her heart of hearts, though, Meg was disappointed in Chuck and resented the fact that he never stood up for her and his child to his parents. Even after they were married and living in their own place, his mother always had that look of disapproval in her eye, blaming her for her son's failure to finish his college education. He had started taking night courses while working as a box boy at the The Piggly Wiggly Market, but it was a slow process.

That Christmas of 1959, their first together, they managed a small table-top tree with tinsel and a few special presents for each other. Meg wrapped them colorfully in old comics from the newspaper and used hair ribbons to tie them up festively. The man who lived downstairs from them, an elderly gentleman, lived alone and sparsely. Meg had occasionally brought him some soup or helped do his errands. Christmas Eve brought a little package at the bottom of the stairs. On it was a card that said, "For Baby Matt." When they opened it up, it was a very large can of peaches. That small gift touched her more than a basket of diamonds. It was a gift from the heart.

Meg was trying to be a good little wife. She wanted to be so different from her own mother. Chuck's mom and grandmother were very good cooks, and Meg was trying to improve her culinary skills. She wanted to cook and sew, and do all those domestic-type things.

One night she found a new recipe for Oriental chicken to be served over fried egg noodles. She thought Chuck might like something different, so she made that for dinner. There was just one problem. Somewhere in the recipe she had missed the part about boiling the noodles before you pan fried them, so she just fried the noodles raw. Poor Chuck needed a catcher's mitt to try to catch all the raw, crunchy noodles that were flying all over the kitchen! They went to bed a little hungry that night, but laughed about it.

Chuck's mother and her own mother were constantly interfering in their lives. It seemed nothing she did was right, no matter how hard she tried. Chuck's parents registered disappointment in her and in Chuck whenever they were together, and it put a strain on their relationship.

Early in 1960, Meg discovered she was pregnant again. She was happy because she loved children. All she had ever wanted was to be a good wife and mother. But it wasn't to be. At about two-and-a-half months, she had a nasty miscarriage, followed by a D&C. That sudden termination and feeling of emptiness and loss was heartwrenching.

People don't react with the same compassion, understanding and love when someone has a miscarriage not like they would if you had a child who died. But Meg felt the loss of that child as though it were alive. She mourned deeply for a long time.

• • •

"Honey, guess what? We're going to move into a

bigger apartment!" Chuck said excitedly as he came home from work that day. "I stopped by the folks' house on the way home, and they've bought a place in the country. They're dividing the old house up into two apartments, one for us and one for Granny Wagner. She'll be on the bottom level, and we'll be upstairs. Isn't that great?"

As much as Meg wanted to live in a larger place, she wasn't too sure how well she liked this arrangement. Along with the apartment, they were given the responsibility of having to live near his elderly grandmother. Meg was beginning to feel a little desperate. Here she was, nineteen years of age, and she felt like a little old lady, dressing in stupid little print housedresses, wearing her hair in a tight little perm, going with all the old ladies to card clubs. It didn't make sense.

Too soon, and against her doctor's advice, in May 1960 she found herself pregnant again. This time, fortunately, things went well, only she got so big she couldn't get in and out of chairs or cars, and she had terrible cravings.

"Chuck, honey, could you run down to the market and get me some Ritz crackers, and maybe some tuna?" she asked one night at around eleven. A few times before, she'd sent him to buy lemons, which she ate like they were oranges, and another time she'd eaten a small jar of mustard with a spoon, like it was ice cream.

Her labor and delivery this time were totally different. More than once, she went into false labor, with fierce and severe pain, spending the night walking up and down the hallways at the hospital, only to discover it wasn't the real thing.

When labor finally began for real, she had nothing but problems. She labored twenty-seven hours, and the pain was so intense she thought she was losing her mind. She swore she'd never come out of it alive or sane. After about twenty-three hours, the doctors realized the membranes weren't going to rupture by themselves, so they brought her into delivery with her feet in the stirrups, and ruptured them with a scalpel. Not long after that, little Johnny was born at 3:00 A.M. on February 8, 1961. This time, toward the end, they gave her some mild pain medications, but not much, since Meg and the baby were both so exhausted.

She hemorrhaged severely the first time she tried to get out of bed, and so had to stay in the hospital much longer than normal. Then she developed mastitis of both breasts, with huge lumps on the right one. One was the size of a golf ball. She couldn't even nurse her baby, her breasts were so tender and sore. She would have to lay Johnny in her lap to give him a bottle because she couldn't stand him near her chest.

Finally home, Meg developed a full-blown case of postpartum blues. At times she lay in deep depression, wondering why she even had Johnny, and the next moment she'd be cooing with delight over her new son. It took a couple of weeks for her to start feeling better physically, and then she really began to enjoy her second child, a precious, precious gift, with his grandpa's sandy hair.

Her relationship with Chuck wasn't everything it should be, either. She had regained her figure quickly, regardless of the weight she'd gained with the baby, but he didn't seem to be very interested in making love. Oh, nothing was wrong. He just didn't seem interested in her. But she was busy taking care of her two precious babies and making a comfortable home for Chuck, and didn't have a lot of time to worry about it.

• • •

"California? We're going to California?" Meg was flabbergasted. "But how…what…?"

Chuck laughed. "It's all fixed. All I do is work and go to school, and you've been busy with the kids. Mom and Dad thought we needed a vacation. They've agreed to pay our train fare for a vacation out to California. Don't you have relatives out there in Huntington Beach? We could

stay with them and take a little holiday for a few weeks—
be tourists and go to Disneyland and all the attractions.
Mom will keep the baby, and we can take Matt with us. I've
already bought the tickets, and we leave next week."

"Yes!" she screamed. "Oh, Chuck, this is wonderful!"

California! Oh yes! She really could use a break from
her humdrum life, and the land of sunshine and oranges
and movie stars would be a wonderful change.

They packed their things and boarded the Santa Fe
Flyer in June of 1961 for a long-overdue vacation. They
both needed and welcomed the change. Little Matt had a
wonderful time on the train, running up and down the
aisles, and staring in wonder at America flashing by. They
spent hours in the bubble observation car. Meg had never
seen anything or been anywhere beyond Freeport and
Rockford, Illinois, and so the vistas of her own country
were like wine to her hungry eyes.

The Rocky Mountains were majestic castles rising into
the cloudy mists as the train crawled along precarious
ledges and in the ravines between them. Farther west, she
was enthralled by the clean, stark beauty of the desert and
its spectacular sunsets.

In Huntington Beach, they stayed with Meg's relatives
and had a wonderful time. They went to Disneyland, took
a train up to Hearst Castle, drove down to Tijuana, Mexico,
and went swimming in the gentle blue Pacific almost every
day. Meg and Chuck fell in love with California.

After they got back home and saw the sharp contrast
between California and Illinois, they quickly made up their
minds to move west as soon as possible. Meg didn't think
she could face another winter in Illinois, and she already
missed the casual lifestyle and ever-present sunshine.
Chuck was working as a mechanical draftsman for
Honeywell at the time, and while they were in California
he discovered he could triple his salary out there in the
same field. They could be independent of their families,
live on their own, and make a fresh start. Meg hoped that

if they got away from all the interference from his mother and her own they might rejuvenate their marriage. Chuck's mother had never felt Meg was good enough for him, and Meg's mother was constantly telling her how to raise the children, how to behave, and still made her feel like she could do nothing right.

They packed their meager belongings, and in August 1961 they piled into their car to begin a new life in California—Matt, a little over two years old, Johnny, six months old, and Chuck and Meg. Traveling three thousand miles with two babies in the car was an experience in itself, but they were young and hopeful, and Meg, with her ever-present sense of humor and zest for life, made it an adventure.

They stayed with Meg's relatives in Huntington Beach once again while they looked for a place to live. Chuck was lucky and found work with North American, a company in Downey, within a week, but finding a house was more difficult. Property and rents were much higher in California than in Freeport, Illinois, and it took much longer than expected before they finally found a small house they could afford to rent in Lakewood in mid-September.

The move to California didn't improve the relationship between Chuck and Meg, as she hoped it would. Her heart was still young, vibrant, and carefree—even after having two babies, she still wanted to dance, enjoy music, and have a good time. Chuck seemed so settled…so mature…so stuffy. He didn't like to go places. He was content to stay home. Worst of all, he just didn't seem interested in her at all, and at twenty, Meg was beginning to feel old and dowdy. She was ripe for any attention shown to her and ready for anything that would make her feel young and exciting again.

• • •

"Meg, the Harrises across the street are having a party

this Friday, and you and Chuck are invited. Why don't you come? You guys need to get out more. Linda can watch the babies for a couple of hours. Just bring them over here and we'll have a drink, then we'll go across the street to the party." Her cousin knew Meg and Chuck hadn't been out of the house for a month, not since they moved, and she thought the party might do them good.

Chuck reluctantly agreed to go, and so they drove down to Huntington Beach. Meg's cousin's teenage daughter would watch the babies while they went to the party.

It was a beautiful, terraced home with a swimming pool in the back. The Harrises had loud, wild parties, and occasionally a young up-and-coming movie star would attend. Their sound system was specially built, and the music blasted throughout the house and around the pool.

Meg was dancing the twist with someone else, but she kept noticing this good-looking guy with a fabulous smile and jet-black hair watching her. She smiled back warmly.

"Would you like to dance?" He cut in and smiled at her. When she looked into his eyes, something snapped. He reminded her of Elvis Presley, and being a big fan of his, she was swept off her feet. Sometimes that happens between two people—it's as if a tangible cord, an electric attachment, is suddenly formed.

"Some party, huh?" he said as he gyrated to the music. His smile revealed perfect, white teeth, and his tan was accentuated by his white polo shirt and creased gray slacks.

Meg danced a little wilder and twisted for all she was worth. He was a great dancer and she wanted to keep up.

As they danced, they continued talking. She found out he was in the Navy and was about a year younger than she was, but it didn't matter.

A slow song came on, and he wrapped her into his arms. His fingertips pressed into the small of her back, sending electric tingles up her spine. He moved her closer and touched his cheek to her temple.

"Where did you come from, angel? I've never seen a

vision as lovely as you around here before," he whispered into her ear.

Meg stammered, "Oh, we just moved here from Illinois. We've only been out here a little over a month. We found a house in Lakewood and we like it a lot. It's sure different from Illinois. The people are so much more open and friendly. My husband's a draftsman and works for North American in Downey and...." She stopped herself, realizing she was babbling.

"Well, I'm glad you're here now. You look like you've moved here from heaven, you're so beautiful," he replied, leaning back so he could give her a good look. "Maybe sometime you'd like to come with me to the Navy base and I could show you around some of the big ships."

She murmured she'd like that sometime. It sounded safe. It was just to see some ships. Meg foolishly gave him her phone number.

Tom started calling Meg all the time. She fantasized about him, moonstruck from the moment she first saw him. They continued to flirt and he continued to make serious moves on her. Being a mother of two, and feeling dowdy and as though all romance in her life had ended, this flirtation was very flattering to her hungry ego, and it went straight to her head. She wanted this excitement and needed to hear these lovely, charming things. And boy, could he pour it on.

One day Tom stopped by the house while Chuck was at work. Surprised to see him there, she almost didn't let him in. "Uh, oh hi, Tom. What are you doing here?"

"I had to see you, Meg. All I do is think about you, night and day. You're the most beautiful, most exciting thing I've ever seen, and I want you, need you so much. I know you're not happy with Chuck. Let me love you, Meg...let me love you now, today."

As he stood on her doorstep, Meg's mind spun. She wanted him right then more than anything. Suddenly, she felt desirable, beautiful, and hot. She grabbed his hand and pulled him inside, closing the door quickly behind him. The boys were taking their afternoon naps, and the house was private and quiet.

He took her in his powerful arms and kissed her, softly at first, and then more demandingly. Her fingers laced in his hair and she kissed him back. His hands began to explore her young body, setting her skin and pulse ablaze. They fell to the floor, fumbling hastily at their clothes, wanting nothing more than to feel each other's bare skin.

"Oh, Tom, yes," she moaned. She felt alive for the first time in months, alive and needed, alive and hungry.

So began Meg's first affair. Maybe it shouldn't be called an affair, just great sex. Addictive, joyous sex. Many days while Chuck was at work and her babies slept, she and Tom would have tempestuous, passionate sex. She felt guilty, but couldn't stop seeing him. She couldn't figure out how she had let herself get pulled into something like that. It probably didn't help that her sex life with Chuck was going through a very troublesome time. They seldom made love, and when they did, it wasn't love—it was more like needing to take an aspirin for a headache. He just did it to get it over with and to relieve the tension.

Chuck seemed to find more pleasure in reading *Playboy Magazine* and getting excited by that, which humiliated Meg. She had one man who just dutifully performed the act of sex and made her feel less than desirable, and another man who made sex an electrifying, fantastic thing. How could she give it up?

Right after Thanksgiving Tom told her he was being transferred to the Philippines for two years. She was sorry to see him go, but knew she didn't love him. He just filled an emptiness, a need within her that she wasn't getting from Chuck.

A couple of months later, in January 1962, Meg found herself pregnant once more. This time, her pregnancy was uneventful, and she had so much energy she felt like going everywhere and doing everything. She used to dress the two little ones up and take them to the Brown Derby in Hollywood for lunch. Once Rita Moreno stopped by their table and commented on what beautiful kids they were and what a perfect little gentleman Matt, at three years old, was.

In April she took the boys to Disneyland. As they came off the Jungle Cruise, they saw Walt Disney himself standing in front of one of the little shops. Meg asked him for his autograph, and after he signed, he asked, "Are those your two little boys?"

Meg replied, "Yes," and introduced them.

"My, what handsome young men you have. Would you like to have a picture of them with me?"

"Oh, that's more than I could hope for."

"Fine. Have little Matt stand here beside me, and I'll hold the little one in my arms, and we'll take a picture." As he started to hand Johnny back, Meg noticed his suit coat sleeve was soaking wet. She could have died! She turned fifteen shades of crimson, but he was so gracious and kind. He just laughed and said, "Oh, don't worry about that. I've got grandchildren of my own." She'd never forget how charming Walt Disney was.

Even though they lived in Southern California, she acted like a tourist. Meg planned trips everywhere, and she and Chuck took the kids with them. Life at home was comfortable. Meg had fun planning little birthday parties for her boys and outings for the family. She baked and cooked, kept everybody shiny clean, and the house spotless.

The only drawback was that their sex life was practically nonexistent and seemed to be deteriorating even further. Like her first pregnancy with Matt, Meg stayed very small and didn't even look pregnant, even when she was nearing full term. Maybe there should have been some warning signs that her marriage was failing, but Meg was having such a good time, enjoying a normal family life with her children, that she didn't put a lot of emphasis on it at the time.

That Easter, while she was still pregnant, her parents

came out for a vacation. They stayed with Meg and Chuck and they, too, fell in love with California. They found out her dad could get a much better job and make more money in California, so they went back and quickly made arrangements to move out in July.

Her dad was fortunate and started work as a tool crib supervisor for North American right away. They stayed with Meg and Chuck for a short while until they found an apartment in Bellflower. Chuck and Meg lived in Lakewood, so there was a little bit of distance between them. And since they hadn't seen each other in a while, things were fairly comfortable between Meg and her folks.

In September 1962, Meg turned twenty-one, and on October 25th she had her third son, Brian. The labor and birth went well, and for that Meg was grateful. Medicine was much more advanced in California, and she was given very mild painkillers throughout her relatively short six-hour labor with Brian. When it was close to delivery, they gave her a spinal block, which was great—no pain from the waist down.

The doctor asked her if she'd like to see her baby being born, and she replied yes, so they positioned a mirror at the foot of the delivery table. She lay there like she was observing someone else and watched her beautiful little third son enter the world.

She'd suffered two tragic miscarriages, and she wanted this baby and prayed it would be healthy. He was perfect, and Meg was overjoyed. It had to be one of the biggest thrills of her life, because she was awake and alert, able to watch the beginning of life. If there was one thing that brought great happiness to Meg, it was her three sons. They meant everything to her. She would sacrifice Chuck, if that's what it came to, but she could never be without her babies.

8

Meg took extra time after dinner that night, applying her make-up with care and brushing her hair in the bathroom until it shone like spun sugar. She reached into the tiny bag and pulled out the black and red sexy baby doll nightie she'd bought at Frederick's of Hollywood especially for tonight. The item had strategic cutouts in all the right places, and was filmy and delicate. After Brian was born last October, she'd dieted and exercised to regain her figure, and at five foot six and weighing 130 pounds, she was slender and toned. It was their fourth wedding anniversary and she was determined to get Chuck's engine running.

Chuck lay on the bed. She lit candles, and the room was

aglow with the soft, romantic flicker of flames. Sitting softly on the bed beside him, she began to kiss and touch him, stroking and rubbing his body. She kissed his sexy Sal Mineo eyelids and lay beside him, her body humming with desire.

Rather than taking his time, savoring the teasing outfit she was wearing, and trying to bring Meg to that pinnacle of explosive satisfaction along with him, Chuck was perfunctory and methodical as usual about his routine, his rhythm, and his release. After it was all over, he rolled over and began to snore.

Meg lay beside him in the soft candlelight, quiet tears running from the corners of her eyes. She felt like a whore.

• • •

She tried throwing herself into her house and her children, but she was growing more and more restless, sick of doing the June Cleaver bit. Maybe she ought to go out and get a part-time job. They could use some extra money, and at least it would get her out of the house and with adults for short periods, away from washing clothes, baking cookies and doing diapers. It was the first part of 1963 and Meg was twenty-one, and felt like she was drowning in her life.

Most of their friends' wives didn't work, and she didn't know what Chuck would think of the idea.

"Chuck, what do you think of me getting a part-time job? It would help with the bills, and I feel like I need to get out of the house once in a while and be with some big people, somebody over three feet tall. I'd try to find something in the evenings, so I'll still be able to take care of the boys and make dinner."

Chuck put down his magazine and looked at her vacantly for a moment. It didn't matter to him, really. "Sure, honey, whatever you want to do."

The next morning, Meg searched through the want ads,

looking for a part-time job in the evenings. She didn't want to be away from her babies, but if she made dinner, she figured Chuck could feed them and get them to bed okay.

There were several ads for part-time work, but only one had the hours she wanted and was relatively nearby. "Honey," she said, showing him the ad, "here's an ad for a part-time phone solicitor in the evenings for the Woodmen of the World. It sounds perfect."

"Woodmen of the World?" he said. "I know somebody who has their insurance, and they think it's a pretty good company."

The next day Meg put on a navy blue dress with white pumps, her red earrings and bag, and put her hair in a French twist. She looked very pretty and very business-like. At their office she filled out an application in the personnel department and was asked to wait.

In about twenty minutes, an attractive older man came out and asked, "Mrs. Wagner? I'm Frank Edwards, the supervisor of our telephone solicitation department."

Meg stood and shook his hand. Although she hadn't had any sales experience, her voice was melodious and she interviewed well, and she got the job. Meg's shift was from six to nine o'clock at night, which worked out well with her home life. Chuck got home a little after five, she'd give him the run-down on what was for dinner, and then she'd leave for work. In a way, she felt like he was relieved she'd be gone at night; she wouldn't be bothering him in the bedroom as much.

Frank Edwards was a fascinating, attentive man. He helped her learn her job, and she was good at it. He was forty, twenty years her senior, but she found him very attractive and charming. If she had to describe his ruggedly handsome good looks to someone, she'd probably say he was a cross between William Holden and Humphrey Bogart. He always dressed impeccably and wore spicy cologne.

They had a break at seven-thirty, and often he would

join her for coffee. Somehow it came out that she and Chuck were having marital problems, and he was kind and sympathetic. He'd met Chuck one or twice and wasn't too impressed.

Sometimes after they got off work, she and Frank would stand outside by their cars in front of the tall glass and steel building and just talk. One evening Frank casually said, "Meg, would you like to have a drink with me?" He seemed quite sincere and not at all threatening.

Meg hesitated. She knew Frank was married, and so was she. She liked him, but didn't want to appear too eager or lonely. She replied, "I'll have to call Chuck and see if it's okay."

She went back inside to telephone home. "Hi, Chuck. Is everything okay? The kids went down okay? Listen, Frank would like to take me for a drink before I come home. Do you mind?"

Chuck's answer was just what she expected. He didn't seem to care what she did. "Sure, go ahead. Just try not to wake me up when you come in."

Meg was perturbed. Why should she bother to tell him anything if he didn't give a damn? She sighed dejectedly as she hung up the phone.

Back in the parking lot, she told Frank, "I'd love to have a drink with you. Chuck doesn't mind. Where to?"

He opened the door to his luxurious car and held it open for her as she slid in. He took her to a small but elegant cafe, where they ordered drinks over a candlelit table. As they talked, he shared some of his own private problems with her.

"I'm married, too, you know, Meg. My wife is a prominent doctor who works at Los Amigos Hospital in Downey. She's a wonderful woman, very dedicated to her profession. She's been in a wheelchair for the past five years, after an unfortunate automobile accident. We share a platonic relationship now, each of us very wrapped up in our own professional careers."

Meg took a sip of her drink and watched the flickering flame of the candle. The soft music playing in the background reminded her of happier times she'd had with Chuck. The nearness of this virile man across the table from her was causing her heartbeat to accelerate, and the skin on her arms was electric from his touch on the back of her hand.

Frank stood up and held out his hand to her. "You look like you're a beautiful dancer. I'd be honored if you would dance with me, Meg." The romantic strains of "Misty" filled the room as she melted into his arms. Their bodies fit well together, her cheek against his masculine tweed jacket, smelling his woodsy aftershave. It was as if all her senses were heightened. She felt like she couldn't keep her wits about her with him so close to her.

His hand pressed against her waist, bringing her closer as he whispered in her ear, "Oh, Meg, you're so young and lovely and desirable. I know you aren't happy with Chuck, and I'm lonesome, too. I think fate must have dictated that we meet, two lonely people who need each other."

Her heart was in her throat. The pounding behind her eyes felt like primeval drums. She leaned her head back to look into his gray eyes, and he bent his head down to lightly kiss her soft, full lips. Meg returned the kiss with subdued passion, her pent-up feelings of youth and desire burning deep within her.

The song was over and they returned to their table. Meg's hands were shaking as she picked up her glass. Frank noticed and reached across the table and took her trembling hand in his. "I want you so much, Meg, that I sometimes feel like I can't breathe when you're around. It's more than just a physical desire, though, sweet Meg. I want to be with you, to have you near me. I want to make you happy. I can't ask for a commitment, because we're both married. Divorce is out of the question for me. I couldn't do that to Julia; it would break her heart. But I need to be with you. I think we could be happy together, if we just give it a chance." He looked deeply into her eyes and she knew he was telling the truth.

Meg thought about Chuck and their life together at home. The only happiness in life she had was because of her children, and she needed more than that. She was young and beautiful, vibrant and alive, and Frank was offering her something she wanted and needed.

They finished their drinks and went to his apartment. It was tasteful and expensive and wonderfully masculine. He lit candles and a fire and brought her a glass of wine. Frank pulled her down beside him on the couch and rested his arm behind her. They stared at the flickering flames, and then he turned to her and kissed her softly on the nape of her neck.

Meg's heart pounded with just that small touch. He reached out with his index finger and turned her face toward his to receive his kiss, long and lingering and full of sweet promise.

As they kissed his hands slowly and teasingly began to release her clothing. He stood up and, taking her hands in his, pulled her up from the couch and over to the light of the fire.

"Let me see you, enjoy you, love the sight of you," he said as he undressed her piece by piece, slowly. She was aflame with desire as his hands explored the curves and hills of her body. Frank was a considerate and experienced lover, bringing her to heights of feeling she'd never experienced. She returned his touches with touches of her own, exciting him with her youth and her neglected, heated desire.

What started out as an affair with a married man turned into a deep love for the most exciting man Meg had ever known. They went out for romantic dinners at quiet restaurants and at fabulous, famous places. He took her on little business trips with him up the coast to Monterey. They shared lunches and dinner, dancing close cheek to cheek. He took her to see *Tom Jones* and many other movies. They held hands and shared popcorn. Silly or sophisticated, they enjoyed every moment together.

Meg never lied to Chuck. She always told him who she was with. She just didn't tell him what they were doing. It seemed acceptable to him that she was with her boss. Was he really that blind? Maybe if Chuck had told her to get her butt home, it might not have gone so far. But he never did. He just didn't seem to care.

Frank took Meg to the Cove at the Ambassador Hotel in Los Angeles for dinner where strolling violinists played sweet, haunting, romantic songs like "Clair de Lune." They had favorite clubs where they knew the musicians. As soon as they walked in, the musicians would stop playing and begin special, romantic songs like "Harlem Nocturne," "Misty," and "What a Difference a Day Makes."

When they made love, his eyes caressed every part of her body, from her toes to knowing where the little mole was under her right breast. He overwhelmed her with intense interest in her as a person. He cared about her feelings, her comfort, her pleasure—was she warm enough, cool enough, was the food all right, were the drinks good, would she like to dance, can I touch you, hold your face in my hands? It was wonderful, and Meg felt young, beautiful and alive for the first time in a very long time.

But Meg was still married, and so was Frank. As much as she loved him, she felt guilty about their relationship. She wondered where this was going and what it was going to lead to, if anything. Her situation at home with Chuck was unbearable, and the only joy her home life brought her came from the babies she loved with all her heart. They meant everything to her. But she couldn't stand living like this any longer. She had to get away, needed some space to think about what to do. She knew she couldn't go on like this.

Meg approached Chuck one night in October after she'd made up her mind. "Chuck, I'm going to take a trip back home to Illinois. I'm going to stay with Cindy, see some of the old gang, maybe see your folks. I need some time to think, get my act together, make some decisions. You know we're not doing so well together, and I just don't know what to do about it."

He didn't object, and so Meg flew back home. She spent hours with her friends, talking over old times. She visited Roy's and the park, haunting her old favorite spots. She knew she couldn't sit on the fence forever. She had to commit to something. She was miserable the whole time, missing Frank so much.

When she came back, she knew that even if there were no future for Frank and her together, she had to make some decisions about her own future. She couldn't go on with her marriage to Chuck with the way things were at home. There was nothing between Chuck and her, and that didn't seem to disturb him in the least. That's what exasperated Meg the most. He never had fought for her, never made the effort to care. He never stood up for her to his parents, to her mother, and even now he seemed disinterested in doing anything that would help keep them together. Maybe things wouldn't have been any different, anyway, even if she'd never met Frank. No matter what was going to happen, she had to resolve the situation. She started talking about getting a divorce.

It was a very difficult time for everyone. They spent that Christmas with her parents, and Meg had a hard time not thinking about Frank the entire time. Frank and Meg continued to see each other, but more openly now. After her trip to Illinois she put a more realistic view on this mad, head-spinning affair. She was still very much in love with him, but she knew it had to end. She referred to it as a love affair rather than just an affair, because she truly did love him with all her heart. Her love affair with Frank lasted for one glorious, happy year, and every time she heard "Harlem Nocturne" or "Misty" she felt a pain in her heart.

In March of 1964 Chuck moved out and Meg was granted a divorce. It was a quiet departure. As usual, Chuck just didn't seem to care much about her or his boys. It was traumatic for Matt, though. One day he came to her, crying.

"What's the matter, honey?" Meg asked him, concerned. She'd seldom seen Matt cry about anything.

Rubbing his eyes and sniffling, he asked her, "Why doesn't Daddy love us anymore?"

She took him onto her lap and folded her loving arms around her son. "Oh Matt, you must never think that your daddy doesn't love you. He loves you all with all his heart. It's just that Daddy and I can't get along. I guess we just don't love each other any more, and when that happens it's hard for two grownups to live together."

He looked at her and asked, "Then why doesn't Daddy come to see us?"

Meg didn't have an answer for that one. She didn't know why. Maybe he was too busy, or maybe he just didn't care, but she couldn't let her son know that.

"Daddy must have his own reasons, sweetheart. He's pretty busy with the new space program work he's doing at North American, and you know he works late sometimes. He comes to see you when he can. Remember when he took you boys to the Griffith Park Zoo?" That had been weeks ago, and they hadn't seen him since.

Her answer seemed to pacify Matt, for he gave her a quick hug, wiped his eyes on the back of his arm, and announced, "Can I go play with Steve? He's got some new marbles—cat's eyes and aggies." And he was out the door.

Although Chuck paid some child support, it was minimal, and now she had three little babies to support and a mortgage to pay. She wanted to find a night job so she could be with her boys during the day, and the only thing she could think of that paid well enough was to be a waitress. She'd worked in restaurants like Capone's in Freeport, so the had a little bit of experience.

In nearby Downey there was a very famous place called the Tahitian Village, a large hotel complex with a renowned entertainment lounge. It had a Polynesian theme, and the waitresses wore long flowered dresses and flowers in their hair. She didn't want a job wearing some skimpy outfit where guys would be after her body all the time and making rude suggestions.

When she applied, the owner asked her, "Have you ever worked as a waitress before? What about a cocktail waitress? The volume and type of customers we get here would be like the Green Room in downtown L.A., or maybe Chez Mario's in Santa Monica. Do you think you can handle it?"

"Oh, sure," Meg replied, and named off a couple of other places she and Frank had visited that she figured they'd never check on. In fact, she'd never served a cocktail professionally in her life, but she'd always been able to bluff her way into something she wanted, and she wanted and needed this job because it paid so well. On the plus side, her striking blonde good looks were working for her, and she got the job.

With the help of a dear, sweet, patient bartender, she quickly learned the ropes of serving cocktails and what it took to make big tips. The pay was minimum wage, but she astutely learned how to flatter people, be friendly, and to give that little extra consideration to make people feel special. She made excellent money.

Her hours were a little crazy, since she worked from 6:00 P.M. to 2:00 A.M. She hired Maria, a live-in housekeeper, to take care of the boys at night, and she was able to be with them all day. Matt was in school, but she was there to pick him up, help him with his homework, and drive him to Cub Scouts. It was tough, but she was making it. The pay was relatively good, and the tips were terrific, especially on the weekends.

She finally stopped seeing Frank because it was too painful. As much as she loved him, she knew he would never divorce his wife. She needed to do something positive to change her life, find a relationship that might go somewhere, not keep hitting herself over the head with a brick. If she kept seeing Frank, she knew her heart would get broken beyond repair.

She became friends with one of the other waitresses, Linda Scott, a single parent like herself, who had a daughter about Johnny's age. Linda had been around the block a few times, and she helped Meg learn even more about the business of being a cocktail waitress.

"Who's that good-looking guy over there, Linda?" she asked one night, referring to one of the bouncers. He'd noticed her, too, but they hadn't had any personal contact.

"Oh, him? That's Vince Moreno, one of our bouncers. Forget about it, girl. He's one sly fox, and has every girl around here following his scent. Don't get mixed up with that one. He's a love 'em and leave 'em kind of guy."

Meg wasn't so sure. Despite his incredible physique and dark good looks, there was something quiet and vulnerable about him. She made up her mind to try to find out more about this intriguing man.

Working at the Tahitian Village was never dull. The acts the nightclub featured were fabulous. Her favorite was a troupe of Samoan fire-knife dancers who would dance to the throb of thundering drums, throwing and juggling sharp sabers and lit torches.

One night, some guy came in and sat on the end of the row of seats in the showroom, watching the performance. He was drinking beer, which didn't cost much—35 to 50 cents a bottle. Every time she served him a beer, he would tip her a buck. She figured she had a good thing going here, bringing this guy beer like it was going out of style. Then when she went up to pick up an order she heard an enormous crash. The guy had fallen out of his chair into the aisle, out cold. "Damn," she said, "there went my big tipper."

She began losing herself in her work. While working at the Village, she struck up a friendship with Mickey. Mickey, a Samoan dancer, was the complete opposite of Frank. He wasn't suave or charming, but he had a boyish,

naive, innocent appeal. Maybe that's why she was attracted to him. Sometimes you run from one thing to the
opposite. She started dating Mickey and they had a lot of
fun together. The only thing was, when they went on dates,
his car reeked of the fuel he poured on the batons he used
for dancing. When they made love, which he was very
good at, she saw that his chest was all scarred from the
knives he used in his act.

Meg had become friendly with the musicians at a few
of the clubs around town, some of whom played at the
Tahitian, and occasionally when she got off work she
would stop in one of the other clubs to see her musician
friends, have a drink, talk and unwind before going home.
One night she went into the Sierra Lounge on Lakewood
Boulevard to listen to her musician friends play some jazz.

"Hi, Artie," she said, greeting the drummer. Still dressed
in her long, Hawaiian dress from work, she perched at the
piano bar and ordered a drink.

Some guy came up and sat beside her at the piano bar,
which was quite low, and offered to buy her a drink.

Tired, Meg politely said, "No thanks, I already have
one. And I'm so pooped that I'm gonna head right out after
this and go home to my kids."

"Aw come on, honey, just have one drink with me.
What would it hurt?"

"No, really. I have to get going," Meg insisted.

He grabbed her arm roughly and looked down at his lap
and said, "I think now you'll have that drink, won't you?"

When Meg looked down, she froze. He had a gun
aimed at her stomach underneath the ledge of the piano bar.
She had never felt such terror, not since she was little.

She sent a terrified look at Artie, and he read it right
away. He put his sticks down, leaned forward and spoke to
Reiber, another musician. They both came flying over the
bar, knocked the guy off his chair, and smacked the gun out
of his hand. Reiber took the gun and sat on the guy while
Artie called the cops.

Artie walked her out to the car and locked her in, telling her to go straight home. Meg was shaking from head to foot. She'd seen some pretty wild things happen at the Village, but nothing this frightening. Shaken, she hurried home, tiptoed in, and kissed her babies softly.

Meg cooled her relationship with Mickey. He was getting too serious and too possessive. She could just see herself five years down the road, barefoot in a thatched hut in Samoa, sitting under a coconut tree, with a passel of brown-skinned babies underfoot. No thanks, not for her. But not dating was unusual for her. She'd always had a man in her life.

She kept noticing Vince, the bouncer at the Village. He was extremely handsome and had a build like Mr. Universe. He must have been a weight lifter to have shoulders and a chest like that. He had dark, curly hair and penetrating brown eyes, quite a contrast to her own blonde good looks. He laughed easily, and what a smile! Meg needed to know more about this hunk, but he seemed so shy, which was part of his charm. She would find a way. She'd talked to him once or twice, but that was it.

The Tahitian Village had two different showrooms, one upstairs and one downstairs. Upstairs was for the high rollers and the big spenders. Big-name acts appeared up there, and the dinners started at $25.00 a plate. Being new, Meg usually worked the downstairs lounge. One night she tripped on the hem of her long skirt at the top of the three steps that led down to the showroom, spilling a whole tray full of tips all over the floor. Vince heard the clatter and came right over to see if he could help.

"Here, let me help you pick that up," he said, kneeling down beside her. "Are you okay?" he inquired solicitously.

"Oh, I'm okay, I just feel a little stupid for tripping like that," Meg responded.

"Those dresses aren't made for going up and down stairs," he sympathized. He and Meg began scooping up change off the floor, and when their eyes met it was magic. Meg's heart was racing, and she kept dropping more money than she was picking up.

Everybody at the Village considered Vince a big playboy. He lived in one of the motel rooms at the Village and had girls coming and going all day. He was currently dating a girl who did modeling with her legs. He was quite the busy guy, so when he started eyeing this little cocktail waitress, the two owners of the Village were pretty surprised. He would be quite a catch for whoever could land him.

At the end of May Vince asked Meg for a genuine date for dinner. "Meg, would you like to have dinner with me next Thursday? That's your night off, isn't it?"

Meg thought, he must have done his homework to know that, and secretly she was pleased. "Yes, Vince, I'd like that very much." Inside, her heart was thumping, and she felt like a schoolgirl being asked out for her first date.

The night of their date Meg waited and waited and waited. After two hours, she presumed she had been stood up, and boy, was she steamed! She was sorry and agitated he wasn't at work the next night, because she wanted to give him a piece of her mind.

She was just sitting down with the boys for lunch on Saturday when the phone rang. It was Vince. She didn't know if she wanted to talk to him, she was so angry, but she decided to hear him out.

"Hi, baby. Listen, I'm sorry I couldn't make it Thursday night, but I guess I had some kind of flu bug. I fell asleep and slept right through our date. Couldn't even make it in to work on Friday. Do you think we could try again next Thursday? I'm really sorry, and I do want to see you."

Meg listened to his pleading voice and relented. "All right, Vince, you're forgiven. But this is the first time in my life I've ever been stood up, so you have to take me someplace especially nice to make up for it. Agreed?"

A week later after work at two o'clock in the morning Vince asked if she'd like to have a cup of coffee. Lee, one of the owners, his wife, Vince, and Meg went into the coffee shop and ordered. As they were talking, a very boisterous, loud guy came in with a drink in his hand. He was being pretty rude to the waitresses and it looked like trouble.

His eyes lit on Meg and he stumbled her way. "Hey, pretty lady, whatta ya say you 'n me have a li'l drink?" He waved his glass in the air, spilling some on her.

Vince went up to him and very politely said, "Excuse me, but it's after closing and you'll have to give me the drink now." The guy refused and became more and more belligerent. Vince again said, "I'm not trying to cramp your style, but you have to give me the drink or we could lose our license."

The guy took a swing at him, so Vince calmly and coolly reached over and grabbed the guy's hand with the glass in it and squeezed it. The glass broke and the guy ended up in the hospital with stitches. The incident had shown Meg the quiet strength within this man.

Vince noticed Meg seemed pretty rattled. "Would you like to come back to my room and have a glass of wine or some coffee before you drive home? It'll give you a chance to calm down."

Meg wiped a shaking hand across her brow. She didn't think she could drive home right now. "Yes, I think I could use a drink."

Vince walked with her through the soft June night to his room, his arm lightly around her waist. At his door, Vince kissed Meg softly with his hands gently around her neck. Meg's head spun and she felt so weak she had to lean against the side of the building. She'd rarely had a reaction like that to anybody's kiss.

He unlocked the door and they went inside. Vince brought her a snifter of Grand Marnier and led her to his balcony overlooking the swimming pool.

"I like to come out here alone sometimes and just enjoy the view," he said. "When it's late and quiet, I can almost imagine myself in some tropical paradise." He turned to look at her, then leaned over and softly kissed her again.

He must have sensed her hunger, for the next thing she knew, he had taken her brandy glass and placed it carefully on the wrought iron and glass table on the balcony and took her in his arms, just holding her with his strong, protective arms around her shoulders and her head resting in the crook of his neck.

No demands were made, no words were spoken, but Meg knew she would make love to this man. Silently, she followed him into his bedroom, where she slipped into heaven. Meg had been having sex for over nine years now, but never, never anything like this. The earth really did move, sending her body into spasms of shaking climax. When they made love, she literally felt as if she were floating on a pink cloud. Like no one else, he did things to and with her that she didn't know existed—wonderful, loving, passionate things. Here she was, a woman of twenty-two years with three kids, and she'd never dreamed that sex and love could be like this. Not even Frank had made her feel this vibrant and sexy.

That first date lasted two weeks. Meg went home every day to be with her boys and play with them, maintain her household and talk with Maria, get some fresh clothing, and then she rushed right back to Vince's waiting arms.

What started out as a physical attraction and passionate sex grew into a deep, bonding love. He was everything she needed, everything that had been lacking all her life. He was passionate, possessive, and he cared about HER, not what anyone else thought or what else was going on. He gave her the strength she needed right from the start, and fulfilled her every need. He was strong physically and emotionally, not afraid to show a quiet, tender, introspective side, a vulnerable side. He was firm yet considerate with her children, fun-loving yet fatherly. He called her "Baby" right from the beginning, never Meg. Life was complete for Meg. She had a wonderful lover and friend, her babies, and a great life.

The only dark cloud on the horizon was her mother. Her parents had moved from Illinois to California to be closer to the grandchildren and, from the moment she got there, her dominating mother tried to run every aspect of her life. Even after the divorce her mother would have Chuck over for dinner each week and do his laundry. Irene would never forgive Meg for divorcing Chuck, who, in her opinion, was the perfect catch. In her mother's eyes, Meg still couldn't do anything right. She never would.

Meg, eighteen months, wearing necklace from real dad

Meg, five years old

Meg, age ten

Meg, age twenty-two

Meg, age thirty-eight

Meg, age fifty-three

9

Little by little Vince moved his belongings from his suite at the Tahitian Village into Meg's house, and they began to feel like a real family. Meg and Vinny were happy and so in love, and the boys were happy, too. Meg wanted to be with him as much as she possibly could, twenty-four hours a day. Everyone was happy except her ex-husband Chuck, and Meg's mother. This was 1964 and cohabitation was frowned upon greatly.

When Vince moved in, Meg's mother called her on the phone. "What kind of an example are you setting for those little boys, bringing that strange man into your home?" she spat. "You're living in sin, Margret Wagner, and you know it!" She still called her by Chuck's last name when she talked to her. Irene nagged her constantly, eternally telling her how immoral she was and what an unsatisfactory person and mother she was.

Was it wrong because she loved someone so much and because he was everything that she needed? Maybe her mother was jealous because at last she had found someone who was strong and fulfilling. Meg didn't know. But every week, Chuck and Irene did everything in their power to lay a load of guilt on Meg to try to make her life as tense as possible.

She and Vince and the boys had a comfortable relationship. Unlike Chuck, Vince was always ready to do fun things as a family with her sons. One trip they'd never forget was another one of his *kidnaps*.

"Should we take the big cooler, or just the little one, Vince?" she called from the kitchen. "Where are we going, anyway? And how long are we going to be gone?"

Vince popped his head around the kitchen door. "This is a mystery trip, woman, so be prepared for anything." He loved to surprise the family by kidnapping them and taking them to places they'd never been before. It was a welcome change for Meg. With Chuck, she'd always been the one to plan outings, figure out where to go, arrange the details, get the tickets and money, pack everything. She liked this take-charge kind of man.

Setting the picnic cooler by the front door, she went to check on the boys and found Vince already in their bedroom, talking with them.

"All right, men, we're headed for parts unknown, so be prepared for any eventuality. Bring your swimsuits and flashlights, jackets and towels, sandals, pillows and popcorn." The boys saluted and then attacked, knocking him over in a tumble of hugging arms and legs.

They ended up at Belmont Shores in Long Beach, where they had a wonderful picnic on the sand. The boys went wading and swimming and Meg and Vince relaxed in the sun.

After lunch was over and packed up, he instructed them, "Okay, troops, into the car. We're headed for adventureland!"

Their next stop was the Pike near the Long Beach Pier. None of Meg's boys had ever been to the amusement area before, and their eyes shone with excitement as Vince led them into the fun zone.

"All right, who wants to go on the Tilt-a-Whirl?" he called out gleefully, waving a handful of tickets in the air.

"I do, I do!" they chorused and sprinted for the ride. Meg sat that one out, and as she watched them spinning around, all crunched in the same car, Vince's arms around her boys, her heart was ready to burst with love and joy. What a remarkable man he was. He treated the three boys as if they were his own, and loved them dearly.

At the arcade, the boys tried their hands at the shooting gallery, basketball hoop throw and darts. Each of them won some small prize, and athletic Vince managed to conquer the harder games to win a big teddy bear for Brian, a walking foam alligator on a stick for Johnny, and a real Indian headdress, complete with colorful feathers for Matt. Tired but happy, they collapsed into their pillows in the back seat on the ride back home.

Meg and Vince quit working at the Tahitian Village; they both felt it would be better for the children and for the family if Vince could get a job with more regular hours and Meg could just be home with her boys. Vince found a succession of jobs as a security guard, a janitor, and even went to beauty school at night. Often it was a monthly struggle to meet the bills, but even when they didn't have much money, Meg made life an adventure. When the utilities got turned off because they couldn't pay them on time, she just made the best of it, eating by candlelight or taking picnic dinners to the park.

Times were tough for a while, and money was scarce. Meals were often a few hot dogs, stretched with beans or macaroni and cheese. The kids liked that kind of food, anyway, and they never knew how their parents were struggling to make ends meet.

They'd been together for several months when in October Meg suddenly started bleeding heavily. The doctor confirmed it was another miscarriage, but this time it was Vince's baby, the baby Meg wanted so desperately.

Vince found her lying in their darkened bedroom when he got home that night. "Are you in here, babe? What's the matter?" he said as he sat softly on the edge of the bed beside her.

Meg's face was buried in the pillow as she spoke. "Oh, Vince, I wanted this baby, your baby, so much. I went to the clinic today because I started bleeding, and I've had another miscarriage." She started to cry again, softly.

Vince leaned over and laid his head on her back. He stroked her arm as he said, "I know, I know. But we'll try again. And just think how much fun we'll have practicing." He gave her a little tickle, and she rolled over. A smile was beginning to form on her face.

"Personally, I don't think you need any practice, but it wouldn't hurt," she said teasingly, tears still glistening on her face.

Vince pulled her into his strong arms. "I'm so sorry, so sorry. You know I love you, baby. It's going to be all right, you'll see."

• • •

Irene's constant, negative recriminations were causing Meg a lot of pressure. Irene had always had a very negative effect on her, but lately Meg was beginning to wonder if some of the things she was saying could be right.

The tension between them was so great that they hadn't spent Christmas with her parents this year, and Meg was sad about that. The boys enjoyed being with Jim and Irene, but she just couldn't take it. She was kneeling in the living room, putting away the Christmas ornaments when she heard the phone ring. Picking it up, she answered, "Hello?"

It was her mother. "Hello, Margret. I hope you had a nice Christmas. Your father missed you, but then, I don't imagine that makes much difference to you. I want you to think about what kind of a message and example you and that Vince are giving to those innocent young children. You and I both know it's wrong to subject my grandsons to your immoral lifestyle. I brought you up right, in the Church. You know you're living in sin and will burn in hell if you don't change your ways."

Something inside Meg snapped. "I don't give a damn what the hell you think. I'm sick and tired of listening to you tell me how to live my life and how to raise my children. It's none of your damn business who I live with or how I live my life!" she screamed into the receiver.

Her mother was not to be thwarted. "I think it is my business, and if you don't listen to me you will regret it."

It was all Meg could stand. She slammed the receiver into the cradle and lost her mind. The Christmas ornaments were hurled against the wall, shattering into thousands of glittering shards. She swept the magazines off the coffee table in a rage, picking up a *McCall's* and trying to tear it in half, succeeding only in ripping the first few pages off the cover. Porcelain figurines of dogs and horses were flung at the front door.

She roared, "Go to hell!" and pulled the now almost bare Christmas tree over on its side and began kicking it. Her rage vented, she fell to her knees, crying and sobbing hysterically, her hands covering her face.

Vince heard the noise from the kitchen, where he was making sandwiches for the boys. They were at a friend's house playing with their new Christmas toys, and would be back in half an hour for lunch. "What the hell...?" He stopped mid-sentence.

When he walked into the living room and saw the destruction, he was astounded. He walked cautiously over to Meg and knelt beside her.

"What's wrong, baby? What's the matter?" He tried to remove her hands from in front of her face, but she lashed out and started beating at him with her fists.

"It's all your fault," she screamed, pummeling him with her hands. "I just can't take it any more!"

He tried to take her in his arms to quiet her down, but she writhed like a woman possessed and began screaming at the top of her lungs, "No! No! NO!!" Her frenzied strength freed her from his arms, and she crouched in a corner of the room, panting raggedly, a wild look in her eyes.

"Baby? Tell me what's going on. What's wrong?"

She wouldn't answer him, just crouched there like a cornered beast. He was afraid the boys would come home and find her like this and would be scared out of their wits. He didn't know what to do. In desperation, he called Irene.

"Irene, something's wrong with Meg. She's busted up the living room and is breathing like a wild animal. She won't talk to me or respond. I think she's having some kind of a breakdown or something," Vince said emotionally, concern in his frantic voice.

Irene called her family doctor right away, and he suggested that they take Meg to St. Francis Hospital in Lynwood to the psychiatric ward. She called Vince back, and he agreed to meet her there. He then called the neighbor and asked her to watch the boys.

She was passive enough as Vince carried her to the car, but as soon as they got to the hospital and she saw her mother, Meg became hysterical and totally out of control. Vince tried his best to settle her down, but nothing worked.

At the sanitarium Irene filled out the necessary papers, while Vince hovered helplessly in the background. Irene turned to him and said coldly, "You may go now. I think you've done quite enough. Just stay away from my daughter and my grandsons."

● ● ●

Meg was sedated so heavily that she didn't remember anything else until the next morning. When she halfway came to, she found herself shackled, arms and legs, to a bed.

"Wha...what's goin' on? Where am I?" She tried to move her hand up to brush the hair out of her eyes and found it chained down. Panic and hysteria set in immediately, and she screamed and thrashed, trying to escape. Again, she was sedated. This went on for several days. Whenever she woke up and found herself restrained, she'd scream and cry, thrashing frenziedly, and they would sedate her. In between, she was a vegetable, a nothing, a zombie with a blank, faraway stare in her eyes. She wouldn't talk to anyone, wouldn't respond to anyone, and didn't want to. She had crawled so far into herself she didn't want to react to or with anyone. She just wanted to be left alone to hide somewhere inside herself.

There was a horrible noise and pressure inside her head. She didn't know how to describe the noise. It wasn't loud, but it was a constant noise with pressure and pain.

She was still heavily tranquilized, but at least this time when she swam up from her drug-induced coma, she was out of the shackled bed. A couple of days later she finally started to react to her surroundings and some of the people there. She could tell she was in a hospital, but there was a gridwork of some sort, bars over the windows. She wore a shapeless gown, something like the hospital gowns that tied in the back, but this was sort of a muu-muu.

She began to respond to her surroundings, talk a bit to the other patients, and now she cried quietly instead of hysterically. She started to eat.

The hospital she was in was one of the best in the country, and Doctors Shoemaker and Hacker were top psychiatrists. In fact, Dr. Hacker had helped the Hearst family when Patty Hearst became involved with the terrorist group that had brainwashed her.

It was a very exclusive sanitarium, and where she was

didn't look much like a hospital at all. Each patient had a private room with comfortable amenities, and everything was painted in pleasant, soothing colors. Good art work was on the walls, and the staff wore pastel uniforms, not all sterile white. It had two sections, one for psychotic patients and one for the *neurotics*, like her. There were pool tables and ping-pong tables for recreation.

Some of the inmates were there not because they were neurotic or needed psychiatric help, but because their rich parents had put them in there to dry out. Two of the guys she met in the sanitarium, Ted Harding and Robin Scott, she got to know pretty well. Ted was the son of a famous entertainer in show business, and Robin's father was a highly placed political figure. They had all the comforts of home in their room, along with a fabulous stereo system. Being in the hospital didn't stop them from getting drugs. More narcotics were smuggled into that hospital than Meg had ever seen. Celebrities used to come to visit these two patients and bring them books which had been hollowed out and filled with drugs. They were having a ball in there, playing the game and going with the program.

Ted and Robin helped her get straightened out. They would sit and talk with her for hours. The three of them would shoot pool, play ping-pong, and listen to jazz music when they had free time. They did a lot of talking and sharing, and Meg felt they really helped her understand her feelings.

"You know what your problem is, man?" Ted told her one day. "You just have to learn not to accept other people's guilt trips. I mean, if they feel bad about something and don't like what you're doing, that doesn't mean you have to feel bad, too. Screw 'em."

"Yeah," agreed Robin. "Like, my old man, he's down on me because I blow a little grass now and then. But look at him. The guy's so tanked up on Black Label most of the time, he doesn't even know what time it is."

Meg had to laugh at their perspective. They were refreshing in their honesty.

"Now take your old lady, for instance," Ted continued. "She don't like your living with your old man, Vince. So what? She isn't living with him, you are," he laughed. "If he makes you happy, what does she have to beef about? Oh, I know the old Catholic dogma and stuff, but do you really believe that you're living in sin? What's a sin is living with somebody you don't love."

Robin agreed. "Yeah, like my dad and mom. She can't stand his guts, and he knows it, and I don't think he likes her too much, either. But a divorce would blow his chances for re-election, and would ruin her social standing, so they stay together in a mutual hate relationship. Does that make sense?"

Meg smiled in agreement. It was sort of like her dad and Irene. Her father didn't show any love to her mother much these days. Why he stayed with Irene, Meg couldn't figure out.

Somehow Ted and Robin had managed to get most of the cute female patients into their beds, and they had sex everywhere they could. Meg couldn't believe the attendants didn't see what was going on—they had sex in the showers, in their room, everywhere.

The doctors still gave her some pretty strong tranquilizers to keep her calm, and twice a day she had intense therapy sessions in her room. Through tests and free association, Meg discovered some of the reasons why she had gone over the edge. Her mother's constant recriminations, stress, and guilt had culminated in a short circuit of sorts. Now it was up to her to better learn how to deal with those kinds of problems—especially her mother. She didn't know if she could.

She didn't know what they were giving her, but sometimes she wondered if the medication was building up in her system. She felt disoriented a lot of the time. One night she picked up her dinner tray at the serving area in the community dining room. Holding her tray in her hands, she walked over to the table, sat down with Ted and Robin and fell face-first into her dinner, nose in her mashed potatoes. They picked her up, cleaned her off, and after that she felt the doctors began cutting down on her medication.

While she was undergoing therapy, Irene came to visit. Meg didn't know it was her mother. They just called her to the visiting room and told her someone was there to see her. When she walked down the hall and saw Irene, Meg totally lost it again, becoming hysterical and running back to her room, angry, frightened and embittered.

All during this time the doctors did everything they could to keep Vince and Meg apart. They wouldn't let him come visit at all, feeling she was too deeply attached to him. She was, but she knew it was a good attachment, and they didn't realize that. Since they kept them apart, he had to sneak notes in to her with visitors who came to see the other patients. He called on the phone and she called whenever she could. But still they were kept apart. Finally, one night Meg couldn't stand it.

"I'm going crazy not being able to see Vince," she told Ted and Robin. "I know it's all my mother's doing. But somehow, some way, I have to get out of here and go see him." She laughed sardonically. "Besides, you guys are making me horny with all your carrying on with the women patients around here. Isn't there any way out of here? Can you guys help me out?"

They came up with a plan. Somehow the dynamic duo bribed an attendant and got a key to unlock the bars on the window in their room. Meg wasn't about to go anywhere without her make-up, so she stuffed eyebrow pencils, mascara, and lipstick into her bra. Ted and Robin created a diversion in the hall, and she quickly jumped out of the second-story window. When she landed heavily on the ground, all her make-up came flying out of her bra, but that didn't stop her. She ran across the yard as fast as she could. She knew at any moment they could discover she was gone. Somehow she climbed the eight-foot chain link fence surrounding the compound and got over the top.

January was usually a rainy month in Southern California, and this year was no exception. When she jumped over the fence and landed on the other side, her shoes went so far into the mud they got stuck solid. She left them and ran on.

She was covered with mud to her knees, but calmly walked to a house near the hospital and rang their doorbell. "My car broke down and I tried to see what was wrong and sure got muddy. Could I please use your phone to call a taxi?" The puzzled good samaritans agreed, and she called a cab to take her directly to Vince's apartment in Downey.

When he opened the door, Vince's eyes opened wide in disbelief. "Baby! Wha...? How did you get here?" His mouth fell open with total shock, and then his strong, loving arms went around her.

"Oh, Vince, I couldn't stand not seeing you, hearing from you, feeling your arms around me. I've missed you so much I thought I was going to die!" She kissed him passionately and held him desperately close to her, never wanting to leave him again. "Make love to me, Vinny. Make love to me and bring me to that pink cloud like I always know you can," she pleaded with tears in her eyes.

He picked her up and carried her into his bedroom. They made love for hours, then they made love some more. To Meg's mind, this was all she needed to get better.

• • •

During her illness her kids had been staying with her mom and dad. Vince couldn't keep them—he wasn't a relative—and there was no place else for them to go. Meg knew Irene was trying to turn the boys against her, and especially against Vince. She'd even told them once that Vince was the reason their daddy had left them, which was totally untrue.

In the small hours of the morning after her dramatic escape, Vince convinced her that she had to go back and complete her treatment.

"You have to go back, baby. You have to find out what made you get so crazy. You have to learn how to deal with whatever Irene dishes out. They'll find you and come and get you, anyway. And when this is all over, we can be together again. You have to get well, if nothing else, for the kids' sake," he reasoned.

She didn't want to leave the safety and comfort of his strong, loving arms, not for a second, but she knew he was talking sense. "Okay, Vince, I'll go back. I'll go back and I'll listen to them, and I'll play their game." Reluctantly, she agreed that what he said made sense. She had to go back and complete her treatment.

They made love again, and Vince held her until the first rays of the dawning sun began to peek through the window. After a breakfast of coffee and kisses, Vince called a taxi, and Meg solemnly held him and kissed him goodbye. In the early morning light, she voluntarily returned to the sanitarium. She'd do anything, even this, so that she could be back home with her Vince and her children as soon as possible.

As she pushed the speaker button at the large wrought iron gate to the hospital complex, her nerves faltered for a moment, but then her natural sense of humor took over. Boy, would they be surprised to see her coming back in here. Dr. Hacker would probably have a fit himself. She couldn't wait to tell Robin and Ted about her adventure.

• • •

One horrid day, Bruce Klinger, a guy she'd become casual friends with, had gone home on a pass to visit his folks. He was in the sanitarium because he was gay and felt so guilty about it he couldn't handle it. His parents couldn't accept his way of life and had had him committed to try to help him. He was getting treatment, but it didn't seem to be doing much good. After he'd returned from his visit to his folks, he became so depressed and upset that he walked out into the hall of the hospital ward, poured lighter fluid on himself, and lit himself on fire.

Meg stood in the doorway of her room, watching the man burn, her knuckles pressed to her teeth, soft anguished cries coming from her throat. The smell reminded her of burned toast, and she was getting sick to her stomach. They put the fire out right away, but he was burned horribly. It was upsetting to the whole ward, and all the patients were rattled that night. Meg thought to herself, it would have been better if he had died.

Meg continued her treatment, and in March of 1965 she was released from the hospital.

Shaking her hand, Dr. Hacker gave her a warm smile. "I think you're ready to go home, Meg. We've delved into some of the reasons why you became so violent, and hopefully you've learned some coping skills to deal with your anger and frustration. I still want to see you twice a week for out-patient therapy. Best of luck." He hugged her briefly.

"Thank you, Dr. Hacker. I appreciate everything you've done for me. And I appreciate your releasing me to go home with Vince. I don't think I could stand living with my mother."

She was on the road to recovery, feeling very good and ready to start a new life with Vince and her boys.

Vince and she rented a beautiful two-story condo in Long Beach and felt at last they could be a family. She had Vince, she was over her tragic nervous breakdown, and soon her boys would be moving in with them. Vince and Meg shopped for bunk beds and furnishings and worked hard to get the kids' bedrooms ready for them.

It was not to be. Before they could even get the cartons unpacked, they had a visit from Chuck and Irene.

Standing stiffly at the doorway to the apartment, Irene stood clutching her handbag beneath her arm. Her dark print paisley dress did nothing to soften her countenance. "Margret, I'm here to inform you that you will not be allowed to bring my grandsons to live here. Chuck and I plan to take you to court to take those boys away from you. This is no way to raise those children," her mother said hatefully. "They need a Christian home and they need their father. You don't deserve to have those children, and if I have anything to say about it, I'll see to it that you won't ever see them again."

Chuck nodded his head in agreement. He didn't especially want them living with him, but he'd go along with whatever Irene had in mind.

Meg stood stunned, unable to speak. Behind her, Vince moved up to put his hand on her shoulder. Finally, she found her voice.

"I don't know what I've ever done to deserve such hatred from you, Mother, but I will tell you one thing. As much as you hate me, that's exactly how much I love my boys. They're everything to me. They're my life and my reason for living. I'll fight you, and I'll win." She slammed the door in her face.

Chuck and Irene filed a lawsuit and followed through with it. Meg was devastated. It's a wonder it didn't throw her back into the hospital, but she had learned a lot through her therapy sessions and had become a lot stronger. And she had a loving Vince to bolster her strength.

On the day of the hearing, there was no doubt in Meg's mind that the judge would hear all the testimony and would give custody of her boys to her. She loved them so much. She went into the courtroom that day with confidence, and she maintained that feeling throughout the hearing, even though Irene and Chuck were telling lies. She felt surely the judge would know what was really going on.

Looking back on it, Meg guessed she must have had an inexperienced attorney, because Chuck and Irene were able to manipulate and twist the facts to make it look like she was an unfit mother. They said she'd had a nervous breakdown and she wasn't getting the proper treatment. That was an out and out lie; she was getting treatment and continuing treatment.

When the judge announced his decision, all she remembered hearing was, "I hereby deny custody of said minors to their mother, Margret O'Conner Wagner...."

Bolting from her chair, Meg screamed at the top of her lungs, "NO!!"

Screaming didn't help. She had lost the three little boys who were a piece of her soul. She was completely devastated. She couldn't live with that decision. She still had Vince and his love and his strength, but she couldn't face living without her children. She loved them with all her heart, and to have them ripped out of her life at a time when she was so vulnerable and still in a recovery process was more than her fragile state of mind could handle. Her mother had betrayed her in the worst way possible. On May 11, 1965, her mother took her children away from her.

10

"Come on, Meg," Vince called as he lit the candles on the dinner table. "I've made poached salmon and au gratin potatoes with a Caesar salad especially to tempt your palate and put some meat on your skinny little bones." He went over to the couch where she was sitting, vacantly watching television, and took her hand in his.

Her constant silence and her lack of interest in much of anything was beginning to worry him. She no longer made the effort to cook, and Vince had been forced to become a pretty good chef. He knew there was something seriously wrong, because she didn't even spend time on her make-up in the mornings, just faced the day with the countenance God had given her, which, lately, was a sad one.

With a sigh she let him pull her up off the couch and bring her to the table. She had no appetite, no interest in food, but she'd try to eat something to please him.

"What do you say we go out to the movies tonight?" he suggested hopefully. "There's a funny Jerry Lewis film at the Strand."

"Sure, whatever," she murmured, not really caring what they did.

Vince was kind and funny, attentive and loving, trying to tempt her with good dinners, both at home and at fine restaurants, suggesting movies, doing everything he could think of to snap her out of the deep depression she'd fallen into. But she just wouldn't eat and didn't have any interest in anything. Her babies had been taken from her, and her heart felt like it was made of ice cold stone.

• • •

Each day followed the next with no distinction, no separation. She moved like a robot in a gray fog, automatically carrying out the activities of daily living to a degree, but not really participating in the whirl of life going on around her.

Meg would stay in the apartment for days at a time without even getting dressed, crying and missing her sons, not believing what had happened. How could this have taken place? How could her mother be so horribly cruel?

It was summertime and school was out, and she often visualized her children out there somewhere, playing and having fun. At the grocery store or at the movies, she'd see a little boy in the crowd who reminded her of one of her sons and she'd burst into tears, sobbing. Looking out at the bright June sunshine made her even more sad. It was too bright, too real. She closed the curtains and went into the bathroom.

Closing the door behind her, she leaned on the bathroom sink and stared at her reflection in the mirror. She thought, why bother? What was there to live for, anyway? Opening the medicine cabinet to get her toothbrush, she saw the packet of Gillette razor blades. Picking it up, she took one out and held it in her fingers, delicately like a glass flower.

Nobody could ever tell Meg that suicide was the coward's way out. It took every ounce of strength and courage she could muster to make that first cut in her wrists. She must have stood in front of the bathroom mirror, looking into her own despondent eyes, watching herself cry, for half an hour or more, trying to make the final decision. She didn't want to go on living, and she knew she'd never feel Vince's arms around her again if she died. But as much as she loved Vince and knew he loved her, the pain of losing her children was too much for her to bear.

Finally, a wave of hopeless suffering swept over her, engulfing her in depression and sadness, and she slashed deeply at both wrists with the razor. In a distracted way, Meg thought, it was a funny feeling when she cut her wrists. The wounds initially felt icy cold when her skin was first laid open. A few minutes later the burning—an excruciating burning sensation—took over, and it was very, very painful.

Time was meaningless as she stood there, leaning on the edge of the sink and staring into her own tortured eyes, her wrists over the sink, while her life's blood dripped away. In a distracted way, she was sorry she'd made a mess that Vince would have to clean up.

When Vince came in the door, he was surprised to find the drapes pulled closed on such a beautiful day. Dropping his lunchbox in the kitchen, he called out, "Baby, I'm home! Where are you, hon?" The apartment was strangely quiet. Maybe she was sleeping again. He walked quietly toward the bedroom to check on her.

Looking into the bedroom, he found she wasn't there. Odd. Where was she?

Bleeding in the bathroom, Meg was starting to get lightheaded and wasn't very coherent when he opened the door. "Oh hi, Vinny," she murmured and fluttered a little wave at him as she began to slide to the floor.

"Oh, my God! What happened?" He caught her before she fell. His hands were shaking and he was in a panic. What should he do? His heart pounded as he assessed the situation. Looking around frantically, he pulled two bath towels down from the towel rack and wrapped them as tightly as he could around her wrists, then picked her up and hurried to the car.

On the way to the emergency room, he kept talking to her. "Oh please, Meg, please don't die. I can't live without you, baby. Oh, why did you do this?" He was close to tears.

At the hospital, they stitched up the slashes in her wrists. Dr. Hacker was notified, and Vince was told to drive Meg to counseling sessions twice a week, but they didn't seem to help. The doctor prescribed some anti-depressants and tranquilizers to help keep her calm.

Too bad the hospital couldn't have taken a few stitches in her broken heart, too. But nothing could heal the wound that her mother had caused when she ripped her children out of her life.

• • •

Weeks went by, and still Meg couldn't shake her deep depression and despair. Irene would barely even let her talk to her boys on the telephone. Once or twice Matt had managed to call her, and she got to talk to him and little Brian, but not for very long. They were always afraid that Irene would come in and catch them. They'd been threatened not to talk to her or call her. Hearing their voices brought joy to her heart, but missing them so much was killing her. Each time they called, it just made the ache in her heart worse. With each passing day, Meg found fewer reasons to go on and saw no purpose in living any longer.

In the past, Meg always tried to make every holiday a special day for her family. On Saint Patrick's Day, she'd make corned beef and cabbage and even tint the mashed potatoes green. For Valentine's day she used special heart-shaped pans to make a double-decker cake with pink frosting. For every holiday, big or small, she got out the boxes of decorations and created a festive atmosphere in their home. The Fourth of July was another special day for Meg and her boys. This year she'd been planning to take them for a picnic at the beach and out to see the extravagant fireworks display at the Huntington Beach pier. But this year she didn't have her children.

Sitting at the dining room table, the sun shining in through the lacy curtains, Meg stared at photographs of her boys on the table before her, pictures from happier times and happier occasions, times when they'd been together as a family.

"Oh, Mother, how could you do this to me?" She knew Irene couldn't possibly love her boys as much as she did. Nobody could love them as much as she did. Irene was only doing this to hurt her. Didn't her mother realize she was also hurting those little boys? They needed her, needed her love, and if Meg had them there with her right now, she'd wrap her loving arms around them and never let them go.

Looking for a way to silence her sorrow, she tried to think of a way she could end this tormented existence. Looking at the stitches on her arms, she didn't know if she could go through the agony of cutting her wrists again. The memory of that pain was only a month old. There had to be an easier, more gentle way to leave this life.

Meg stood up and went to get her purse. She took the bottle of valium out and carefully set it on the table. Going to the cabinet beside the sink where she kept the good glasses, she chose a crystal goblet, then rummaged in the box of everyday medications and vitamins, looking for the bottle of phenobarbital. She put that on the table next to the Valium. Next, she poured a glass of orange juice from the

Frigidaire and sat down at the table, lining the vials up on the kitchen table like twin guardians.

Opening the Valium, she poured four into the palm of her hand and threw them to the back of her throat, washing them quickly down with a gulp of juice. Again and again she swallowed, quicker and quicker, anxious to get them all down, anxious to find peace and an end to the ache in her heart.

It was hard to take so many pills. She started feeling full and sick, but she didn't want to throw up the pills she'd already swallowed. Maybe what she'd taken already would be enough. She was already starting to feel a little groggy. Staggering to the bathroom, she shakily put on fresh lipstick and then went to the bedroom to lie down. This time she would be presentable, at least.

Once again, she don't know if it was an intuition or what, but Vince found her before it was too late. He'd come home to take her to her appointment with Dr. Hacker, only to discover the remnants of her fatal feast on the kitchen table.

"Oh, Jesus," he muttered, hastily searching the rooms for Meg. He found her on the bed, looking beautiful and serene. "God, Meg, please don't be dead!" he prayed and checked to see if she was breathing. Yes! She was still alive!

"Come on, baby, let's get up. It's time to wake up now. Come on, get up." He put his arms around her and propped her up in bed. "Coffee...I've got to get some coffee in her."

He ran to the kitchen and started some coffee brewing, and quickly mixed up a cup of instant with hot tap water. It looked like mud, but he forced it down her.

While the coffee brewed, he walked her, dragged her, back and forth, up and down the short hallway of their apartment, around and around the coffee table. Vince didn't want to call Dr. Hacker, because he was afraid that, with this second attempt on her life, the psychiatrist would inform Irene, and they'd probably want to put her back into the sanitarium. Vince knew that would kill her.

Meg threw up several times, not always in the bathroom. Vince didn't care; at least it got rid of some of the barbiturates. He kept pouring coffee down her, talking to her, walking her for hours and hours. Finally, she seemed alert enough and out of danger, but still he kept her awake, talking about the good times they'd had, trips he was planning for them to take, telling her how much he loved her. Eventually, she fell into a deep, natural sleep in his arms. Once again he had saved her poor, pathetic life, a life she no longer wanted or had any use for.

• • •

Meg tried to snap herself out of it. Even though she didn't have her children, there must be something left in life worth living for, some purpose she could find to make her want to stay alive. She tried to concentrate on Vince and how much he loved her, and for a while things seemed to get better. She no longer sat in the apartment with the drapes closed for days at a time, not bothering to get dressed in the morning and not caring about anything at all. She started taking better care of herself, fixing her hair and make-up, going out with Vince once in a while. But not too often. She still cried when she saw children who reminded her of her own three lost boys.

The fall weather brought cooler days, for which Meg was grateful. It was hard to wear long-sleeved shirts to hide her scars when the weather was hot. September had always been an enjoyable time for her. September brought her birthday and Matt's, and she loved planning his birthday party celebration. She liked taking the boys shopping, getting Matt ready for school. She'd always buy something for Johnny and Brian, too, so they wouldn't feel left out.

In a few days it would be her twenty-fourth birthday, and Matt would turn seven just two weeks later. She remembered some of the birthday parties she'd planned for him and his friends, and her heart ached. Once they'd had a cowboy party, where all the guests came dressed like Roy Rogers and Hopalong Cassidy. She'd even made a cake that looked like a cowboy hat. What would Irene do for his birthday? Meg never remembered any parties being given for her, and she hoped that Matt wouldn't miss it too much.

When she'd gone into the hospital, her mother had told her she would take care of her children until she was well, but on that day in court Meg remembered Irene's hateful words.

"You'll never get these children back. A misfit mother like you doesn't deserve them. The court has given me custody and I plan to raise them right."

Meg was looking through their photograph album. There were pictures of her as a little girl, even one of her First Communion in her beautiful white dress. There were pictures of her parents, Irene grim and Jim with a smile on his face. Pictures of her and Chuck when they first moved to California were next, and pictures of the babies when they were little. Her heart was aching to hold them again. She felt like her heart was shattered in two. Half of her was missing in the form of three small boys so dear to her heart.

The razor hadn't worked the first time, the pills didn't work the second time. This time she didn't have to stand and contemplate. She just went into the bathroom and got out the razor blade. Now, instead of just making one cut on each wrist, she figured if she slashed her forearms lengthwise with the razor blade she would bleed quicker, faster, and this time she'd be sure she was successful before anybody could find her.

She slashed as fast as she could. She ended up with more slashes on her left arm since she was right-handed, and they were much deeper. The blood flowed down her arms and dripped onto her shoes and the white bathroom rug.

Maybe it was God's protection, because she was certainly doing everything she could to end her miserable life, but once again Vince found her and rushed her to the hospital. Again they stitched up the severe cuts. Once more she lay in the hospital bed, wishing Vince hadn't found her, wishing she could die.

Each time she attempted suicide, it was as if Vince sensed she was going to try something irrational, because he always rescued her at the last minute. Each time he was the one who made the long, heart-wrenching trip to the hospital with Meg nearly dead beside him.

Each time after he found her, the tears would roll down his face and he would cry his heart out, begging and pleading with her, "Baby, oh please don't do this. Oh, baby, I love you so much. I need you so much. Please don't do this to me. Don't do it. Live! Dammit! Live!"

It was cruel what he was going through, the deep pain that Meg had inflicted upon him. And still he stayed. During this time, he was the only one who knew what was going on, who knew about her suicide attempts. No one seemed to question why, even in the heat of summer, she wore long-sleeved blouses, sweaters and large bracelets. It was Vince who had to cope with and live through this horrible tragedy, trying to give her the will to live, trying to love her hard enough to bring her back.

Vince tried everything to get her interested again in life, trying to improve her spirits. He'd talk to her for hours about their future, painting a picture of possibility and hope. Finally, she began to believe that maybe if she got her act together, they might conceivably have a future. With his help, she started trying to struggle through.

They wracked their brains, trying to think of a way to improve their lifestyle and security, some way to make enough money to convince the court they were stable and secure. Meg planned to appeal to the court to try to get her sons back.

"Bingo!" Vince exclaimed, putting down his pencil. He was surrounded by papers and folders at the little desk in their bedroom, where he'd been sitting every evening for the past week. Meg was reading in bed and looked up with a question in her eyes.

"How'd you like to own a beauty shop, my dear?" he asked out of the blue.

"A what?" She'd often been to beauty shops, but knew nothing about running one.

"There's a beauty shop for sale for a ridiculously low price in Downey, and I think we could make a go of it. Back in 1960 I went to beauty college so I know how to run that type of business. Oh, baby, it might be just the thing to pull us out of this slump."

Meg put down her book and thought hard about it. It sounded appealing, and it was something they could work at together, which would be fun. She was tired of staying home and doing nothing. Just maybe they could make it work.

Vince crawled across the bed and started showing her papers and explaining his ideas. "We could call it the Satin Doll," he said excitedly.

"Okay, let's go look at it in the morning."

A few weeks later they opened the Satin Doll in Downey. Vince was an excellent hair stylist, and taught Meg how to assess a woman's hair texture and face shape, cutting and styling to flatter any customer. She learned the intricate science of coloring hair and giving permanents that looked natural, not kinky or frizzy. Meg established her own little corner in the salon where she would give facials and do make-up for the ladies, and this became a profitable part of the business. Gradually, they hired other hair stylists and a manicurist.

As with any new business, it was hard to get going, and cash flow was a problem, so Vince found a job driving a beer truck, delivering beer, to bring in a steady, reliable income. Meg worried daily about Vince's safety that steamy August of 1965, because some of his delivery routes for the beer companies took him dangerously close to the riots that were destroying South Central L.A. He carried a gun, and Meg prayed he would never have to use it.

Meg was still depressed, but was too busy to let it get her down. Still she missed her children. One night after the salon closed, Vince and she were cleaning up and getting ready for the next day.

"Hey, baby, how would you like a shampoo on the house?" he teased. He knew there was nothing like having someone else wash your hair to make you feel relaxed.

Meg jumped at the chance. He wrapped a towel and protective cape around her neck and she sat in the shampoo chair. His fingers massaged her scalp, and Meg purred. As he rinsed her silky blonde hair clean with the spray of warm water, he bent down and kissed her softly.

"Meg Moreno...," he mused. "Don't you think that has a nice sound to it?"

Startled, she sat up, water streaming down her face. "What did you say?"

"Baby, I think we ought to get married. I love you so much, and I know you love me, too. It would make a big difference to the court, and maybe to Irene, if we made this legal. With the Satin Doll doing pretty well, if we get married, we'll prove to the world that we can be good parents. Somehow we'll get the kids back. It's going to be a long struggle, but we can do it."

Meg never expected Vince to propose to her like this. "In reference to your first statement, my answer is yes, yes, YES! Oh, Vinny, I love you!" She threw her arms around him and, wet as two cocker spaniels, they held each other tight.

Meg had no choice but to believe him. It was either end her life or put some faith in what he was telling her.

While she ran the salon, Vince delivered beer all over Los Angeles County. They did what they could to build up their financial security, sacrificing new clothes, entertainment, and all luxuries to put money in the bank. They had to prove to the court that they were financially and emotionally secure so she could try to regain custody of her babies.

• • •

Irene still wouldn't let the boys come over to visit, claiming that Vince's presence was a negative influence. Meg began to blame some of her problems on him. There was no one else to take it out on. In November of 1965, she got in one of her frustrated, depressed moods again and packing her bags, she left Vince, thinking she was going to try to get him out of her life. Everything else was all screwed up, why not get that straightened out, too? Maybe if she wasn't with him, her mother would give her kids back to her.

She hid out in Orange County with some friends. Vince was frantic; he didn't know where she was. The whole time she was gone she couldn't eat or sleep; all she did was cry. Now she missed not only her children, but the one man in her life who loved her and whom she loved desperately. She knew in her heart she couldn't live without him.

Finally, she called him, told him where she was, and asked him if he would come and pick her up. Meg knew she'd put Vince through hell that year. Yet through all of it—her breakdown, the suicide attempts, her desertion—this man had stayed with her, taken care of her, and loved her. She didn't know how he kept his spirits up and why he stayed in love with her, but he did.

After they got back together, things between them seemed better than ever. She'd had time to think, and she knew in her heart that although things weren't perfect between them, she couldn't live without him. They started making plans to be married.

11

Meg's green eyes sparkled with love as she and Vince stood holding hands in Irene and Jim's apartment in Bellflower. She was radiant in a long beaded pink dress with a matching hat. Her satin high heels had been custom dyed to match. Vincent was handsome in a tailored dark suit. In her hands, she carried a simple bouquet of peach lilies and white daisies and baby's breath. It was December 11, 1965, at 6:00 in the evening, and Vincent Moreno and Margret O'Conner Wagner were getting married.

It was a simple ceremony with just the immediate family in attendance. Meg was proud and happy to have her children there. All three of them had a part in the wedding ceremony, each with a job to do. Matt held her bouquet at the critical part of the ceremony, and Johnny carried the ring on its special little pillow. Brian was proud to be the one to scatter the flowers on the carpet before she walked proudly out of the bedroom to the living room to meet her new husband.

Doctor Hacker had convinced Irene that marrying Vince would be a positive step for Meg's continued recovery, and he had urged Irene and Jim to have the wedding at their apartment and allow Meg's children to attend and participate in the ceremony. Irene was dead set against the idea.

"Whether you like him or not is irrelevant, Mrs. O'Conner," he'd told her bluntly. "Your daughter is an adult, and in my opinion, Mr. Moreno is good for Margret, and he seems to care for her very much. Meg seems to need him, and I think this marriage is a positive step on the road to her further recovery."

Irene and Jim weren't overjoyed about this. Irene hated Vince, and Jim didn't like him all that much, either. The two of them pretended they were at the wedding, but Meg knew their hearts weren't behind this union. Oh well, at least they were making it legal.

After the ceremony, her boys crowded around her, bursting with pleasure at seeing her again, and excited at being a part of the wedding.

Matt came up to her and gave her a hug. "You look so pretty, Mom. I've never been to a wedding before, especially not when it's my parents."

Meg had to smile at his words. She quickly caught on to his reference to Vince as his parent, too. The kids were happy that she and Vinny were getting married. All three boys knew that Vince cared for them deeply, and they liked him and thought he was fun.

Her father put his arm around her and took her aside privately. "You know, Meg, I always thought it was a mistake when you divorced Chuck, but I know I can't be the judge of what happens behind closed doors in a marriage. Frankly, I think Vince is not your type. He's unskilled and he's rough around the edges. But if he makes you as happy as you tell me he does, then I wish you the best of luck. All I want for you in this world is for you to be happy." He kissed her on the forehead and gave her a squeeze.

Meg's eyes misted with tears. "Thanks, Daddy. That means a lot, coming from you. I just wish Mama felt the same." More than anything, Meg wanted her mother to accept Vince, to give him a chance to show her what a decent human being he was.

Before she left, Irene had a few words to say, too. With a tight look on her face she came over to Meg. "You know, Margret, in the eyes of the Church, you are still married to Chuck. This marriage is a farce, and it won't change my mind about your relationship with this Vince."

Meg turned her back on her, not willing to let her ruin this, the happiest day of her life. She looked up at her handsome new husband with her eyes shining with love and joy. He loved her and she loved him, and they were good together. He accepted her for herself, and he gave her the love and support she needed.

On the way back home to their little apartment they had a flat tire and it was pouring down rain. Their life together had certainly gotten off to a crazy start, but she didn't care. They didn't have time to take a honeymoon trip, as they both had to get right back to work the next day, Meg to the Satin Doll and Vince to deliver beer, but this night was their wedding night and it was magical.

"Vince, do you feel any different?" she asked as she removed her hat once they got back to their apartment.

His was a typical male response. "Not really, baby. But I'm glad we finally decided to make it legal. Why? Do you feel different?"

She smiled her quirky smile and looked shyly at him. "Well yes, a little. I feel a little like we're starting fresh, starting over, somehow. Sure, we've been living together for a while, but getting married…this is the beginning of something special, something new and wonderful."

"I'll show you something fresh, Mrs. Moreno, if you'll just come over here closer to me." He pulled her near and gave her a hungry kiss.

That night they danced lovingly in their living room by candlelight to a tune that was to become their song— "When A Man Loves a Woman" by Percy Sledge. If nothing else, they knew they would always have each other, to have and to hold from this day forward.

• • •

Vince and Meg tried very hard to make a success of the Satin Doll. It was tough, though, to get a new business going, and for some reason the customers just weren't coming in. Prices were high on supplies, and things weren't going well at all. Before long, they found themselves behind in their taxes on the salon, and late in 1966, the government closed them down for back taxes. It was a good thing Vince still had his job driving the beer truck.

They scraped by on his salary, and Meg was continually looking for some type of a job she could do to help pull in some additional income. Late in May of 1967, she saw an ad in the paper for a make-up girl for the beauty salon in the May Company in Lakewood for Ahnee Cosmetics. She circled it in red and showed it to Vince.

"Do you think I should try for it, Vinny? It says experience necessary. I don't have any sales experience, but I'm pretty good at working with make-up." She'd always loved to fool around with hairdos and make-up, ever since she was a child playing with dolls.

Vince read the ad and handed the paper back to her. "Baby, this ad was written just for you. You always look gorgeous, and besides, you've had experience in running the Satin Doll. You can always put that down on the application. You've been selling beauty for a long time, and you're a walking advertisement for your own expertise."

The next day she spent over an hour getting her make-up just perfect. She wanted to look totally perfect, but not too made up. The style was dark eyeliner and light-colored lipstick, and it took time to get the effect just right. She carefully blended several colors of eye shadow to make her green eyes look large and exotic. Dressing in her peach suit, which complemented her striking blonde good looks, she set out to apply for the job. After filling out the application, to her surprise she was asked to stay for an interview.

The cosmetics department manager asked her, "Have you ever had any experience selling make-up before?"

Brave Meg bluffed yes and proceeded to tell her about it, embellishing her work at the Satin Doll. She was good at applying her own make-up, and had done make-up and facials in the Satin Doll on occasion, but that was the extent of her experience. To Meg's total amazement and delight, she got the job.

Selling make-up was easy for her, and she loved it. She regarded herself as something of an artist, using a woman's skin and bone structure and applying her paints and liners to coax the beauty inside to appear.

In the Ahnee Cosmetics make-up booth at the May Company she would give ladies complimentary facials and apply their make-up for them, the idea being that they would buy the products she had used on them. She quickly became the top make-up salesgirl in all the May Company stores.

One day in September a distinguished-looking man approached her counter as she was arranging a promotional set-up. "May I help you, sir?" she asked politely. "We're having a special promotion this week. If you purchase one of our new eyeshadows, for an additional ten dollars you can receive this attractive make-up kit that contains samples of many of our products. Perhaps your wife would like this as a gift."

He appeared interested and she moved to the chart of skin tones. "Now what color hair and type of complexion does she have? We have colors to enhance every woman's beauty."

He smiled and said, "Actually, Mrs. Moreno, I'd like to introduce myself. I'm Mr. Adrian, the owner of Ahnee Cosmetics. I've come from New York, and I've been doing some studies and projections on our cosmetic line here in California. You're one of our top sellers and a beautiful woman, too, I might add, which is great advertising for our product. I'd like to make a proposition to you. I'm looking for someone to supervise all my make-up stations in the beauty salons in all the May Companies in Southern California, and the Macy Stores in Northern California. You'd be training the make-up artists and also the sales-girls behind the counters. Naturally, your salary will reflect the added responsibility, and with the position there would be an expense account and a company car. I know this is a lot to take in all at once, but please think about it."

Meg was stunned and couldn't say a word. She just stared at him like he was an alien from Mars.

"Mrs. Moreno?"

"Um…I…uh, I would be happy to take the job, Mr. Adrian," she said shakily. Could this really be happening? What a wonderful opportunity! "Would…would you mind if I sat down for a minute? I'm a little overwhelmed by all of this."

He smiled and helped her to one of the make-up stools in front of the counter. "Why don't you go home and discuss this with your husband? The position would involve some traveling and being away from home from time to time." She nodded in understanding.

"If you could let me know by Thursday, I'd appreciate it. We have a big campaign coming up to promote our new spring line, and we have to get going on it right away."

Finally, she found her voice. Breathlessly, she turned to him and reached out her hand to shake his. "Mr. Adrian,

I am honored and flattered by your offer. I can almost guarantee that I can accept the job. It's a great opportunity and I know I'll do a great job."

As soon as he left, she ran to the phone in the employee's lounge and called Vinny. "GUESS WHAT!!!" she screamed.

Vince held the phone away from his ear. "Baby? Is that you?"

"I've been promoted!" she said excitedly, and told him all about her conversation with Mr. Adrian. "It'll mean being away from home sometimes, but it's a fabulous opportunity. Oh, honey, what do you think?"

"I think you should take it. Wow! My little Meg, a supervisor! Congratulations!" He could feel her excitement humming through the receiver. "It sounds wonderful, and I'm very proud of you."

The pay was incredible, and it was a very glamorous job. She appeared in publicity stills and magazine ads and traveled everywhere between San Diego and Monterey, San Francisco and Oakland. Business meetings with Mr. Adrian were held in some of the finest restaurants in San Francisco like the Trianon and Omar Khayam's.

After one of her trips, Vince met her at the International Hotel at LAX for dinner. After they ate, they sat and had quite a few drinks, enjoying their reunion and listening to the beautiful violin music. Maybe it was a few too many drinks…in her euphoria, as they left the restaurant, Meg took off her high heels and decided to frolic on the beautifully landscaped lawn and dance through the flowers. It was great until the automatic sprinklers came on!

She enjoyed flying all over the state, traveling and seeing new places and meeting new people, but still she had this awful ache inside, missing her kids. Even though there were a lot of positive and enjoyable things she liked about her wonderful new job, the negative part was that she was gone a lot, away from home and Vince and her boys.

When she was home she was allowed to see them once

a week, times she treasured and held dear to her heart. When she was on the road, she tried to call them as often as she could, but when she was out of town, she missed them terribly.

That September of 1967 was Matt's ninth birthday. When Meg called to talk to him on his special day, he started crying.

"Oh, Mom, I miss you so much. Why can't we just come home and live with you, Mommy? Grandma is all right, but she's awful strict. We can't have our friends over, and we don't play games or get to do sports or anything. We have to be quiet all the time, because she sleeps so much. I miss you, Mommy, and Vince, too. Please, can't we just come home and live with you?" His tearful voice broke her heart, but there was nothing she could do about it.

• • •

Although the quality of the Ahnee cosmetics was good and the public response was positive, unfortunately, the cosmetics didn't sell as well in the stores as the owner had hoped, and the company folded in February of 1968. It had been great while it had lasted, but now she was out of a job.

All this while Meg's children were still living with her mom and dad. Meg went over to her parents' to visit them as often as she could. On the up side, she was able to spend much more time with them now that she wasn't working.

Meg was beginning to be worried about her boys, and even about her mother. A few times when she'd visited during the day, it was more than apparent to her that her mother was abusing prescription pills, and drinking a lot again. Irene spent most of her time in bed, day and night. She'd get up, take pills, wash them down with a beer, and go back to bed. The boys pretty much took care of themselves, and Matt was like the substitute parent. Her dad was working two jobs and wasn't around very much to witness what was going on.

One day she decided to talk to her ex-husband about it. "Chuck, we need to talk about our boys. I'm worried about Mom and her pills and drinking." She paused to gather up her courage. "Whenever I go over there to visit, she's asleep or in a stupor, and she's got pills everywhere in the house. The place is a mess, and the boys seem to be fending for themselves and taking care of her, too. You know I can't talk to her, but maybe she'll listen to you."

This was something Chuck didn't want to hear. He didn't want to take his kids to live with him, and Irene seemed to be doing all right taking care of them. "Oh, come on, Meg," he said tersely. "You probably just caught her on a bad day. She's never been real healthy, and she's no spring chicken, either. She's doing fine, and so are the boys. Just relax and let things alone."

Meg knew there was nothing else she could do to convince him right then, but she resolved to keep a closer eye on what was going on over there. Oh, if only she could have her babies back. She'd give them a loving home and raise them under an umbrella of sweet motherly care.

One night in May she got a hysterical call from Matt. "Mom, you need to come over right away! Grandma fell down in the kitchen and there's blood everywhere!" He was sobbing hysterically and she could hear the other two boys crying in the background, too.

"Is she breathing?" she asked urgently. "Where's Grandpa Jim?"

"He went bowling at the King Pin with his friends, and won't be back until ten," he sobbed.

"Did you try to call your father? Isn't he home?" Meg queried, getting frantic now.

"No. Mom, hurry! I need you here. I don't know what to do! I'm so scared," he sniffled.

"Okay, sweetie, you just keep Johnny and Brian out of there and put a towel under her head. Vince and I will be right over."

Irene had gotten so stoned on painkillers she had fallen

backward in the kitchen and hit her head on the edge of the kitchen table. She had a serious gash in her scalp and was unconscious when they found her, but still breathing. Vince and Meg rushed Irene to Lakewood Hospital. Meg kept trying to contact Chuck and her dad. Finally, at around eleven o'clock, she was able to reach them, and they met her in the emergency room waiting area.

Meg was concerned about her mother, but she was also furious with her. She paced the floor in the waiting room and addressed her anger to Chuck and her father.

"Do you know how dangerous this could have been for the children?" she ranted, gesturing with her arms as she paced. "Mom's usually so zonked out on her downers, it's a wonder she even knows where she is. Most of the time she just lies there in bed and ignores them. What kind of life is that for young boys? How can you tell me she's taking good care of my children?" She flashed an accusatory look at Chuck and glared at her father.

Chuck was silent and looked away, but Jim said, "Oh, Meg, Irene hasn't been feeling well for a long time now, and she just needs to get her rest."

Meg spat, "Rest? She has no business trying to take care of growing children in her condition. It's just not right. Until she gets out of the hospital, I'm taking them home with me. There's essentially nobody there to take care of them during the day while you work, and Chuck's gone, too. They're coming home with me. And don't you try to tell me any different!"

That same night Vince and Meg took the kids, a few clothes and their pajamas to their little apartment. It was too bad such an unfortunate event had to bring about their reunion, but Meg didn't care. She had her boys with her again and that's what mattered.

• • •

The next few days while Irene was in the hospital, she

kept pointing to her throat, unable to speak. It was as if she had a severe case of laryngitis. The doctors finally decided to do some X-rays and found that she had swallowed one of her rings, a large, jagged cocktail ring. After she had fallen, she had put her hand to the back of her head, getting it covered with blood. And even then, she'd tried to take more pills. The ring had slipped off her hand, slick with blood, and she'd swallowed it. It took minor surgery to recover it.

Even Chuck could finally see, and now had to admit, how unsatisfactory the situation at her parents' house was and he agreed to let Meg and Vince take the kids. Vince was earning a decent living, and they had a nice apartment with room for all three boys. Deep in her heart, Meg believed he knew it was the right thing to do, and he knew how desperately she wanted them back.

Shortly after the Fourth of July, Chuck called her with some shocking news. "Meg, can you meet me at my attorney's office next Monday? I've been thinking pretty hard about this, and I think the boys would be better off with you. Your parents are getting on in years, and Irene definitely seems to have a problem with pills. The kids are always asking to go live with you, and maybe that's the best thing for them. I've decided to have my attorney prepare the proper documents and turn custody over to you and Vince."

Meg could hardly believe her ears. The very thing she'd wished for, prayed for, almost died for, was finally coming true. "Oh, Chuck, I...." She had to swallow the lump in her throat before she could go on. "Yes, we'll be there. What time?" He gave her the address and the time, and she went to her important papers box to dig out the documents he told her to bring. She was so excited that she didn't stop to think carefully about exactly what he'd said.

That Monday in Mr. Powers' office, Meg got the shock of her life. Reading through the paperwork she had to sign, she turned to Chuck in astonishment and anger.

"According to these papers, my mother never had joint custody of the boys with you, Chuck. You had sole custody the whole time!"

Chuck shifted uncomfortably in his chair. "Well, yes, but I couldn't have them living with me. You know I travel a lot on my job, and I'm gone all day at work, so when she offered to take them, I agreed."

All this time her mother had told Meg that she had legal custody of her kids. She'd even gloated over it and told Meg what an unfit mother she was. Now Meg discovered Irene never had joint custody with Chuck, at all. Chuck had been granted sole custody of her children, and her mother wasn't even mentioned in the legal documents. Irene had perpetrated that lie just to hurt her, as always. Meg was furious. As she signed the papers that day, she vowed never to let her mother hurt her or control her again.

On July 11, 1968, Meg got her beloved children back, a little more than three years after Irene and Chuck had ripped them out of her life.

What would have become of those innocent boys if her spiteful mother had raised them? What would have happened to them if any of Meg's suicide attempts had succeeded? Meg hated to think about that.

Now that they were a family of five, they started looking around for a bigger place, a place with a big back yard for the kids to play and someplace close to a good school. Vince found a beautiful home in Lakewood that they were able to rent at a reasonable price. At long last Meg had Vince, her three babies, a comfortable house in Lakewood, and her life and her future should have looked bright.

• • •

Meg had endured so many painful and emotionally damaging traumas in her twenty-seven years that she'd begun trying to find comfort in the bottle—a bottle of booze or a bottle of pills. It didn't really matter which, comfort was comfort. Her mother abused prescription drugs, and the inclination was probably there. Meg felt like she had it under control, though. She and Vince would only drink one night a week, on the weekend, but when she did drink she couldn't quit with just a few. She had to finish the bottle, she had to drink until she was absolutely numb. It was a way of hiding so much pain.

With the added members to the family, Vince's paycheck didn't stretch as far, and things were a little tough. Meg wasn't working, as she was home with her young children.

This was to be their first Christmas together in a long time, and Meg wanted to make it extra special, but the Christmas of 1968 was looking a little sparse.

Out of desperation, and with his usual ingenuity, one day Vince threw a rake and a hoe and shovel in the trunk of the car and said, "I'm not coming back until I land a couple of gardening jobs."

When he returned several hours later, he'd managed to contract a couple of hamburger stands to do the landscape maintenance on during the weekends, and that provided a little extra steady income. From those couple of hamburger stands, Vince's landscaping business mushroomed, and they became quite secure financially for the next five years.

• • •

Vince staggered in carrying a big cardboard box. "Hey, everybody," he called, "I have surprise for you!" When he put the box down in the kitchen, they all came running. Inside were two of the cutest puppies Meg and ever seen.

"Dogs?" she said. "Where did they come from?"

"One of the guys at work is moving back to Texas and had to find homes for these two little guys. It was either that or take them to the pound," Vince explained. "I didn't think you'd mind," he added sheepishly. "The back yard has a great fence, and me and the boys will walk them every day. I promise. One's a golden retriever, and the dark one is sort of a shepherd mix. Gee, Mommy, can I keep them?" Kneeling by the box, he looked up at her like a little boy who'd found a couple of strays and brought them home.

Meg laughed and said, "Well, okay, but you have to take care of them like a good little boy." She thought back to her own childhood and to the many years when she'd wanted a pet, but Irene would never let her have one, claiming pets were messy, full of fleas, and ate too much.

Vince worked hard at his thriving landscape business, and Meg helped at home, doing the billing and paperwork, making up flyers and advertisements. But always, they made time for fun, too. True to his old habits, Vince occasionally planned a kidnap vacation, but this time Meg was in on the planning. Twice a year, in February and August, they would take a vacation trip when the landscaping business was slow.

Meg's cousin in Huntington Beach worked for an accounting firm that did some business for Circus-Circus in Las Vegas. They were planning a trip in February of 1970, combining business with pleasure, and asked Meg and her family to come along.

"Why don't you come with us? The hotel will comp us adjoining suites, and it'll be a ball," her cousin Marilyn urged. Marilyn was somewhat of a gambler and flew back and forth to Las Vegas frequently. Amazingly enough, she was either very lucky or very good at cards, because most of the time she managed to walk away from the poker and blackjack tables ahead of the game.

Meg protested, "What'll we do with the kids and the dogs? Besides, I don't know how to play those games. I guess I could always sit and play the nickel slots."

"I'll teach you how to play poker. You just have to learn how to keep your face still when you get something good. The slots are a sucker's game. They're all rigged, anyhow. At Circus-Circus there's a whole floor devoted to games for kids like skee-ball, water rifles, and more, and they have real circus acts going on all the time. We took Linda there when she was about Matt's age and let her just go play the games by herself. It's perfectly safe. Matt can watch Johnny and Brian while we relax by the pool. They have a kennel for the dogs and everything. Please say you'll come, please? And bring something nice, just in case we go see a show."

Since the rooms would be free, they decided it would be fun to go. And the buffet meals at the hotels were famous for serving lots of food for practically no money. Besides, they hadn't had a family vacation in nearly a year.

Ever since she was thirteen, Meg had been one of Elvis' biggest fans. Meg wanted to go see his show while they were there, but when they tried to get tickets, they found that it was sold out; the line went around the block.

Seeing the disappointed look on her face, Vince had a brainstorm. "Come on," he said, and dragged her right up to the showroom where a sign read "Invited Guests Only." He flashed a huge wad of money to the maitre'd, and the next thing Meg knew, they were seated in the third and fourth seats from the stage, right up front. Meg thought she was going to die of joy. She even got to touch Elvis's watch. Vince had never seen anything like it—women running down the aisles from the back of the showroom at the Hilton, acting like love-crazed teenagers. The screaming throughout the show was incredible. As loud as it was during the show, that's how quiet it got when the show was over and Elvis left the stage. It was as if no one wanted to move, let alone get up and leave the room. Elvis was at his peak, and he put on one hell of a show.

• • •

Vince expanded his landscaping business to include large commercial projects, hiring crews of men to do the maintenance and a supervisor to run things when he was gone. Some of his clients were even some of the big hotels in Palm Springs and industrial complexes in Mission Viejo.

In the summer of 1971 the family went to San Diego for a week. Meg wanted to visit historical Balboa Park and beautiful La Jolla, with its galleries and exclusive shops. They took the kids to the San Diego Zoo and spent a day at Pacific Beach and Belmont Park, the amusement park there. They stayed too long at the beach and got so badly sunburned they could hardly walk.

"Oooh, just sitting down makes the backs of my legs feel like I'm tearing the skin back there," Meg complained. They were back in their hotel room at the Bahia and none of them felt much like going out to dinner. They couldn't even get shoes on because the tops of their feet were so sunburned.

"Would you put some of this aloe vera lotion on me, Mom?" Johnny asked, his arms stuck out at his sides like a scarecrow. Nobody even tried to put clothes on, deciding instead to remain in their swimsuits for the evening.

"I think we should order room service tonight. Okay, guys?" said Vince. "I know I don't feel like getting dressed to go anywhere. My clothes would probably feel like sandpaper."

They ordered hamburgers and French fries with soft drinks and lay on their stomachs on their beds to eat and watch TV. That night there was a hilarious Jerry Lewis movie on, and they all had to try not to laugh too hard because it hurt too much.

On that same trip, they drove farther south to a motel in Ensenada, Mexico for a two-day stay. Meg thought the exposure to another culture would be interesting for the boys, and she wanted to do a little shopping in Mexico, too. They were appalled at the poverty but delighted at the prices, and Meg came back with gifts of leather for most of her family, along with some lovely pieces of silver jewelry and duty-free perfume.

That night they ate at a pleasant seafood restaurant,

where strolling musicians played while they ate. Johnny kept tipping the guys with change from his pockets, and so they kept staying and playing and playing. When they went back to their room to get ready for bed, Matt went in to brush his teeth. Something was wrong with the faucet and it wouldn't turn off, and it kept running and spraying a stream of water.

When Vince went down and told the front desk, they told him, "Sorry, Señor, eet is too late to call the plumber. Eef you would like, we will move you to another room."

Not wanting to listen to the water dribble and run all night, they picked up their suitcases and paraphernalia. It looked like a pajama party with the five of them in their pajamas, trooping down the hall to a different room.

• • •

Meg was a careful housewife who shopped wisely and watched their budget, and with Vince's big new landscaping jobs, they were able to put money in the bank. Lakewood was becoming very crowded and built up, and she began to notice the influence of a gang element, both in the schools and in their neighborhood.

"Vince, I think we ought to consider moving to a better neighborhood. The boys are at an impressionable age, and I'm worried about the way our neighborhood is going downhill. We need a better area to raise the boys, someplace where they can meet nice kids from good families."

Vince agreed, and since he had several large contracts to the south, they started house hunting in that direction. In July of 1973, they bought a beautiful two-story, 2800-square-foot home in Mission Viejo. Vince's landscaping business was thriving and growing, and Meg got busy decorating their new home with beautiful new furniture, carpets, and drapes. Meg checked the ads, looked in the used furniture section, and watched every sale. She was proud of the way it turned out. She even took up gardening, buying *The Sunset Garden Book* and studying it in the evenings.

For the first time in her life, she felt the pride of ownership and creativity in providing a beautiful home for Vince and her three boys. They had to budget carefully to afford all the things they wanted, but life was comfortable.

She still drank too much and used prescription drugs too much, but Vince's love and the love for her children kept her going. Their future looked bright.

Meg and Vince liked to surprise each other, and one of the things they both loved was beautiful jewelry. On special occasions, they would shop carefully and purchase quality pieces from reputable jewelers, not only for their beauty but as investment pieces that would hold their value. When Vince and Meg were married, he gave her a wedding ring with one solitaire stone in the ring. Over the years he'd added one or two small stones to Meg's ring on each anniversary. Her ring had become quite a sparkler, and she was very proud of it.

Meg still tried to make the kids' birthdays very special days. She baked homemade cakes of their choosing, whatever flavor or frosting they wanted, no matter how strange the request. One time she even made a green cake with blue frosting. It was ugly as sin, but it made Matt happy. They could request and get whatever they wanted for dinner, be it pizza, pot roast, or fried chicken, and she'd make it from scratch. She wanted them to feel their birthdays were very special days, that this world was a better place because they were born.

She and Vince used to plan special evenings at home, nights when Meg would fix the kids hot dogs or T.V. dinners, while she prepared a strip steak or ground sirloin for her and Vince, with baked potatoes, and a special dessert for them all. She must have learned fifty ways to make something fancy with Jell-O. After the kids were in bed, they would drink and play games, drink and listen to music, drink and make love.

The important thing was they were a family. Her sons were with her, and they would never be taken from her again. Vince had been like a father to them since they were small, and he loved the boys as his own.

There were many times when it was difficult for Vince and for the boys, since their minds had been poisoned against him by Irene and Chuck. The boys often resented Vince when he'd have to discipline them, and they couldn't understand that he had taken on a very difficult task. It's hard enough for a step-parent, even under the best of circumstances, but Vince had an uphill battle. He did the best he could, and truly loved those three boys.

12

Meg was puttering in the garden, tying up tomatoes and beans, when Matt came home from school. She loved the magic and promise of life the earth held, and wherever they lived, she had a garden. This year she'd planted melons, tomatoes, and several varieties of flowers so she'd always have fresh flowers in the house.

"Hey, Matt, you hungry?" She'd just baked a bunch of oatmeal raisin cookies for the kids' lunches, his favorite, and whenever she made them he'd usually wolf down at least half a dozen with a quart of milk at a sitting.

He came to the kitchen door and leaned against the jamb. "Oh, I dunno, Mom, I'm not too hungry right now. Maybe I got a little flu bug or somethin'," he said, swiping at his bloodshot eyes. He pecked her on the cheek and headed into the kitchen.

Concerned, Meg followed him inside. Washing her hands at the sink she asked, "How'd that history test go today? How about I make you some sandwiches to take with you to work?"

He dropped his books on the kitchen table and headed for his room. "I'm gonna hang out in my room for a while before dinner, okay?" he muttered, not answering her, and shambled off down the hall.

Meg was becoming increasingly worried about her eldest boy. He just didn't seem like himself lately. Maybe puberty and being a teenager was different for boys. She didn't have too much experience with that sort of thing, not having any brothers, and Matt was her eldest. She'd have to ask Vince about it.

Matt always seemed so tired and distracted. He spent a lot of time in his room, keeping to himself and listening to loud music. His usually acceptable grades were falling, and he didn't seem interested in very much of anything, not even girls. He'd been dating that nice Diane Taylor down the street, but even Vince had remarked how lately Matt hadn't been bugging him to drive him and Diane out on dates.

Oh well, he was probably going through some sort of phase. Just this last year he'd grown his hair out to shoulder length and had started wearing old, worn-out Levi's and white tee-shirts, quite a change from his previous almost ivy-league look. But then Matt was his own individual and didn't tend to go along with the crowd. He'd always been sort of the quiet one, enjoying his solitude. Meg rather enjoyed these traits in him, and respected his privacy.

The following week as she was putting away some of his clean underwear, she found an ornately carved small wooden box tucked in the drawer beneath a few of his tee-shirts. She'd never seen it before, and curiosity got the better of her. She knew she was prying, but she had to know what it was. The box itself was beautiful, inlaid on the top with mother-of-pearl, and it looked expensive. Maybe it was a gift from Diane.

When Meg opened the lid she gasped and had to sit down quickly on the edge of her son's bed. Inside the box were pills of various colors and small glassine envelopes with white powder in them. There was some leafy material and some Zig-Zag rolling papers which she knew had to be the makings for marijuana cigarettes.

Everyone always thinks, not my kid. Never having had any experience with illegal drugs—she'd abused alcohol and prescription pills, but never experimented with drugs nor wanted to—Meg hadn't recognized the signs and symptoms in her son. But here it was, right in front of her face. What should she do now? She carefully put the box back in the drawer and decided to talk to Vince about it that evening.

"Dope?" he said, stunned. "Matt? Are you sure?"

She told him about the box and then said, "Maybe that's why he's been acting so strange lately, so dopey and tired. He doesn't seem to have any interest in anything, and he spends an awful lot of time alone in his room. Oh, Vince, what are we going to do?"

Vince's first reaction was wanting to beat the crap out of him, but Meg convinced him they should talk about it with him to find out what was going on. Vince wanted to confront him that very evening. "Now Vince, don't get excited," she cautioned. "I want to have a chance to talk to somebody, find out more about these drugs and what they can do. I'm totally ignorant about this stuff. Besides, let's give him a chance to talk to us. Let's hear what he has to say for himself."

They called him into their bedroom two nights later and shut the door. Meg held out the box and said, "Matt, we'd like you to tell us about this."

At first he looked surprised, but then he got defensive and angry. "What were you doing? Snooping around in my room? That's my property. Give it back to me!" He reached for the stash, but Meg quickly handed it over to Vince.

"Matt, I don't know what's going on with you, but we're worried about this. You know that doing drugs is not only illegal, it's risky. You could get in a lot of trouble with the police. The people who sell drugs are dangerous people, people who could hurt you. The drugs themselves are unsafe, too. I'm guessing that's cocaine in that little envelope. Sometimes the dealers put strychnine and other substances in street drugs to cut them, and you never know what you're getting."

Meg paused and then pleaded, "Oh, please, Matt, you've got to get rid of this stuff and stop using it, for your own sake. Your grades are falling, and I can see what it's doing to you. You aren't acting like the son we used to know, and we miss you."

Matt glared at them both, then turned and bolted from the room, slamming out of their bedroom and out of the house.

After that there were almost daily conflicts—arguments between Matt and Meg, between Matt and Vince, between Vince and Meg. The strain in the household and on their marriage was an almost palpable thing, like a dark, hideous beast crouching in the corner in the dark. When drugs come into a family, it tears them apart.

A week after Johnny's thirteenth birthday in 1974, Matt came home exceptionally late. Angry and frustrated, Meg decided to confront him. They had established a curfew and were trying to help him straighten out, but he defied them at every turn.

"Matt," she called, following him down the hall toward his bedroom. "Just a minute, I want to talk to you."

The minute her son turned around, she could tell something was wrong. His eye was cut and his jaw was swollen, and he looked like a bulldog that had gotten into a fight and lost.

"My God, Matt! What happened to you? Are you all right?"

"Oh, I just fell down and hit my jaw, Mom. I think it's just dislocated. I'll be all right."

Meg ran to get Vince from the living room. Vince gently examined Matt's jaw and could tell it was more than just a dislocation. "We're going to have to go to the hospital," he said. "I think it's broken."

Matt's jaw had to be wired shut to heal. The doctors told them he'd have to be on a liquid diet for at least six weeks, at which time they would evaluate how well the injury was mending.

When they brought him home from the hospital that night, Matt was in terrible pain. It tore Meg's heart out to see him suffer so, but there was nothing she could do for him. Meg prayed to God to give her the pain. She couldn't bear to see her child in such agony as he lay there, moaning and even trying to swear between his clenched and wired teeth.

After they got him settled into bed, she sat beside him, her hand on his back, just touching him softly. With her heart and her love she tried to will the pain away. She didn't know if he could sense all the love and comfort she was trying to pour into him with her touch, but it made her feel better to sit there and touch and hold him.

• • •

Meg thought that after his jaw had been broken, Matt would settle down. The weeks he'd spent recuperating were quiet and calm, almost like when he was younger. They played games at night, went to the movies and watched TV together, and he got along better with her and Vince and his brothers. But the brief interlude of peace didn't last long.

As soon as he was better, the trouble started up again. He defied curfew, and Meg suspected he was stealing money out of her purse. In October she got a call from Mr. Solomon at the Bubble Bath Car Wash where Matt worked after school, and he told her Matt hadn't been at work for almost a week.

"Mrs. Moreno, I like Matt and he's usually a good worker, but I need to know that I can depend on him. Would you ask him please to give me a call? If he doesn't want this job, I'll have to find somebody else, and in a hurry."

Meg didn't know what to do. Again there was a conference with Vince, during which he accused her of being too soft on him. "You never do anything to him when he does something wrong. You just slap him on the wrist and tell him he's been a bad boy, and then he goes right out and does it again," he yelled.

"Well, at least I don't yell at him all the time and make him feel like nothing. He's really confused right now, Vince, and he needs all the love and support he can get." Whenever any of her boys did something wrong, she always tried to make them feel that although she might hate what they did, or disapprove of their actions, she always loved them as persons.

Matt went back to work at the car wash, and for a couple of months, the tension in the household was at a bearable level. He was usually in the house close to curfew time, and there was no more missing money from her purse or Vince's wallet. But they had started hiding them in their bedroom, and not keeping much cash available.

Trying to involve him a little more in the family, she took Matt shopping with her to help pick out a gift for Vince's birthday in April. Meg had been eyeing an exquisite pinky ring for Vince at Jessop's and had been putting money aside for nearly a year, paring a little here and there from the grocery money and wherever else she could. It was a thick gold band, hand cast using the lost wax process, with a large rectangular sapphire set in the center.

"What do you think, Matt? Vince has always wanted a pinky ring, and it would make a nice gift from you and me, together. I've saved some out of the grocery money, and if you wanted to give me some of your car wash earnings we

could make it a special present from just the two of us." She
figured if she had him contribute to the gift, it would instill
a little more responsibility and pride in her son.

Matt looked at the ring in the window. "Yeah sure,
Mom, that's a good idea. He'll love it."

For the next few weeks there were no conflicts over his
drug habits or his breaking the rules at home. Matt worked
hard at school and at his job, giving his mother some of his
paycheck to help buy the present for Vince.

But around Easter the beast was back. No matter what
they tried, Matt was angry and defiant, creating arguments
in the family between himself and she and Vince, and also
building stress with his brothers. Brian, her baby, was
starting to show signs of following Matt's pattern of
substance abuse, and she'd found evidence that he was
smoking pot. God, she didn't know if she could handle a
repeat performance and deal with the confrontations that
came up almost daily.

When she went to get the ring they'd bought for
Vince's birthday out of Matt's drawer where they'd hidden
it, it was gone. "Matt," she asked him when he got home
that night, "did you move your dad's present? I wanted to
wrap it today, but I couldn't find it."

Matt shot a startled glance at his mom and then his eyes
dropped to the ground. He turned and bolted into his room,
slamming the door.

Meg followed, flinging the door open and demanding,
"Matt, where's that ring?"

Staring defiantly at her now, he said, "I took it back,
okay? I needed the money, so I took it back."

"You took it back?" she yelled. "God damn it, Matt. I
paid for more than three-quarters of the cost of that ring and
saved a long time to get it for him. What right did you have
to just take it back? Where's the rest of the money?"

"I told you, I needed the money," he said evasively.

"You better think of something better than that, young
man," she thundered. "And I expect you to repay me for

every penny of it, if it takes you the rest of your life." She backed out of his room, slamming the door so hard that cracks appeared in the drywall. She was furious. Her son was out of control, and he was causing her to lose control. He was using drugs, he had lied to them, and now he had basically stolen his father's birthday present and hocked it for drugs.

The next night Matt didn't come home at all. Meg figured he was just pissed off, and so was she, so she didn't even try to find out where he was. She figured he was probably staying with one of his friends. But when he didn't come home for a second night, she began to call around to his so-called friends, trying to find out where her son could be.

One of his buddies at the car wash finally told her. "Matt decided to thumb it back to see his gram and gramps. Someplace in Illinois, I think," he informed her. "Said he'd be back in a month or two."

Meg was beside herself. Her sixteen-year-old son had disappeared, hitchhiking two thousand miles away, without even letting her know anything about it. Frantically, she called Chuck's parents in Freeport and asked if he were there.

"No, we haven't seen him," Chuck's mother said. "Is he coming for a visit?"

"Just ask him to call me when he gets there, okay?" Meg pleaded. "I just want to know that he's all right."

By the time Matt finally did call several days later Meg was frantic with worry. She was relieved to know that at least he had arrived safely, and wanted him to come back home.

"Mom, I don't want to come home right away," Matt stated. "I'm going to stay here with Grandma for a while, maybe try to get things figured out. I'm sorry about the ring and I'll try to pay you back."

"I'm not worried about the ring, Matt, I'm worried about you," Meg cried. "I just want you to be safe and happy, that's all. I'm sure we can figure out a way to solve some of these problems we've been having if we all just give it a try."

Meg talked to Chuck's mother, and she agreed he could stay with her for a couple of weeks, but then asked that they come get him. "I'm too old to have a teenager living with me," she explained. "I'm happy to have him for a while, but he can't live here."

Two weeks later, Vince and Meg and Brian and Johnny piled in their Pontiac and drove back to Illinois to get him. The reason for making the trip wasn't the greatest, but they enjoyed getting there. Vince had installed a citizen band radio in the car, and all of them had lots of fun on the road, talking with other CB owners and truckers.

"Pink Panther to Rodeway, come in," Meg called, addressing the big truck in front of them.

"Pink Panther, this is Black Dog, read you, over."

"Any sign of Smoky up ahead?"

"Nope, clear as a bell," the trucker responded.

Meg figured that CB radio saved them from getting at least a dozen speeding tickets on that trip out and back to Illinois.

They stayed with her old friend, Cindy, and went to see Matt at his grandmother's every day. Meg was amazed at how little Freeport had changed in the last fourteen years. It was the same small town with the same small town people, and she was doubly glad that she and Chuck had decided to move to California. At the end of two weeks, Meg and Matt's grandmother convinced him to come back home with them.

The trip home was not pleasant. Matt sat silent and morose most of the way, refusing to join in with the shenanigans and the silliness. He seemed to be in his own dark world, and nobody else could get in.

• • •

Back home, Meg felt her world collapsing in on her. They were having problems with Matt and Brian, and Vince was gone almost all the time, working hard at keeping his landscaping business going. She felt overwhelmed and depressed by the pressure of everything.

Once in a while, just to get out of the house, she'd drive down to a neighborhood bar, just to have a drink and some adult companionship and conversation while the kids were in school.

One beautiful day in May of 1974, Meg sat in Hennessey's, seeking solace and some peace in a glass of bourbon. Two seats down from her, a man in white slacks and a navy blue pullover sweater had his eye on the gorgeous blonde with the long, tanned legs.

"Hi, can I buy you a drink?" he asked, sliding onto the bar stool next to her.

"Sure," she answered. He looked nice enough. The way he was dressed, he looked like he should be on a sailboat someplace in Newport, and she liked his tanned good looks.

"You look like you just stepped off your yacht," she remarked. "You know, my husband and I have always wanted to own a sailboat. When the kids are grown, we plan to get a forty-footer and sail to Catalina and all around." They started talking about sailing and sailboats. She and Vince had always wanted to own a sailboat, and they already had a boat slip in Dana Point—no boat, just a slip, ready for the day they would someday buy their boat.

Talking to this man, thirty-three-year-old Meg began to feel attracted to him. She wondered if she was still desirable. After all, she had three nearly grown sons, and had been a stay-at-home housewife for a lot of years. Would anybody else still want her, or was Vince the only guy who would stay with her? To boost her ego, she started flirting with this guy she'd never seen before. Naturally, he ate it up and figured he had a good thing going. Meg was still a beautiful woman, blonde and tanned and trim.

After a few more drinks, she was beginning to like this guy a lot more. "Hey, you wanna go down to the marina in Dana Point and see our boat slip? We have a slip, but no boat," she giggled.

It was her own fault. She asked him to go. Funny what drinking will do. It was a short drive to the marina in the warm summer evening and, after looking at the boat slip, he drove them over to a deserted beach area.

"C'mon, honey, les' get friendly. You know you want it. You wouldn'a brought me here if you didn't." He pulled her to him as he fumbled with his belt buckle and took down his pants, putting her hands around him, forcibly trying to make her do what he wanted her to.

The cold ocean air started to sober her up, and suddenly she came to her senses, wondering what she was doing here. "Aw, no. I don't think we better. I gotta get home," she said, pushing him away.

He held her harder, pushing her head down toward the front of his unzipped pants.

"No!" she cried. "I said I want to go home!" She fought him as much as she could, but then he became violent. He slapped her hard, knocking her back onto the sand and quickly knelt next to her. He grabbed at the front of her blouse, but Meg rolled over and tried to get away. Again he snatched at her, pulling at her collar and jerking her back, choking her. She kicked backward and got him in the stomach. Finally, gasping for breath, he gave up.

Doubled over and holding his belly, he muttered, "You ain't worth this, bitch. Get in the damn car." He drove like a bat out of hell to the bar where he had picked her up and practically threw her out. With a squeal of tires, he screeched out of the parking lot, leaving her standing there alone and humiliated.

She sat in her own car a long time, sobbing in fear and shame. What if he hadn't stopped? How could she do this to Vinny? What if the guy had killed her? She started the car and, with tears running down her face, headed home.

Guilt, shame and remorse flooded over her. She picked up some speed and then, blinded by her tears, lost control and crashed into a cement bridge abutment, totaling her car and knocking herself unconscious.

She came to in the hospital being treated for bruises and cuts, with a tearful, frightened Vinny standing over her, once again finding his Meg hurt and lost.

How could she explain to Vince why her clothes were all full of sand and why she was so beat up? She knew she had to…she'd always been honest with him. Even after all she'd put him through, still he stayed and still he loved her.

• • •

May 5, 1976 was a day she'd regret for the rest of her life. Matt was still rebellious, defying them about everything, refusing to honor curfews, still hanging around with a bad crowd. When he'd get home late, he'd just climb up the balcony and come in through his patio door. He was seventeen now, and it was hard to make him conform to the rules that they expected him to follow while he lived at home.

That night Meg decided to teach him a lesson. She decided to lock the door to his patio, forcing him to come to the front door to get in the house and then she and Vince could confront him. His behavior was tearing the family apart, and they had to figure out a solution, something to bring some peace.

He didn't come to the front door. That night he ran away from home for a second time. For days they didn't know where he was, or how he was. They finally got a call that he was staying with his father in Bellflower.

Chuck called and told her, "That kid is crazy wild, Meg. Last night he stole my new Porsche! I tried to chase him down in my neighbor's car, but he cracked up my car and now he's in the hospital. Since you can't seem to control him, I've pressed charges, and the cops have him in custody. He's seventeen now, and it's about time he faced the music. They're bringing him to trial on June third."

Meg was horrified. How could his own father put Matt in jail? She had to do something to help him.

She and Vince went to see Matt in jail in Downey where he was being held, but the police wouldn't let her see him, saying she'd have to wait to see him at his court appearance. Meg felt like it was all her fault.

At the court appearance, Chuck did indeed press charges. Matthew was remanded to the authority of the State and sent to Chino, where he spent time at the Youth Authority. Meg went up to see him as often as she could, even though it broke her heart. She felt degraded every visit. The police even searched her purse and her body before she was allowed to see her son.

Vince and Meg continued to battle for Matt in court, and were finally able to get him released to their custody. Maybe a miracle would happen. Maybe he'd be grateful that they got him out of jail and he would shape up.

He didn't. Things went from bad to worse. He ignored curfew, laughed at their rules, and soon the dark beast of drugs and defiance filled their home once again. There were fights almost every day.

She and Vince were at their wits' end. "What are we going to do?" she sobbed. "Yesterday the Watsons next door accused him of breaking in and stealing their television set. They didn't catch him, but somebody saw a kid who looked just like Matt going into their house. I didn't know what to say to them. I want to believe it wasn't him, but something inside me tells me otherwise. God, Vince, it's awful when you believe your own child is actually capable of something like that."

Vince put his arm around her. "We're doing everything we can for him, baby. But he's the one tearing this family apart. Poor Johnny cries himself to sleep because of the fights that go on every night. I know he's your son, and I know we've been trying everything, but I think he's beyond our control."

Meg wiped her eyes and considered what Vince had just said. She had to face the fact they couldn't handle him. She realized she would have to take him back to juvenile hall. It was the toughest decision she'd had to make in her life.

The drive from Mission Viejo to Los Angeles in late July to turn him over to the authorities was the longest drive she'd ever made. When they got inside the building and she handed him over to the bailiff, a cry came out of her throat that she'd never heard before. It was the sound of a wounded mother lion whose cub had been killed, slaughtered by inhuman means.

Matt shot her a look that made her feel like she was killing him herself. She knew he'd never forgive her or understand why she had to take him back, but she had no choice. Somehow the rest of the family had to survive.

• • •

With all the trouble with Matt, Meg nearly lost control of herself again, being under such tremendous stress. Her two younger sons suffered greatly because of what was going on. Not only did they see what their older brother was going through, but they had to put up with Meg's moods and increased drinking.

Many nights when Vince and she would be drinking, her emotions would get the better of her, and she'd cry and get hysterical and throw things. Once she got so drunk she fell into a coffee table, breaking the table and everything that was on it. She blamed Vince for the hurt and pain Matt was giving her, crying and screaming at him, calling him names. She had to blame somebody, and Vince was the closest one, so he received the full brunt of her anger.

Not many men would have put up with all the disobedience and defiance he got from Matt, who wasn't even his own son. People were interfering in their lives, and even Meg, instead of turning to him, turned against him, arguing and swearing at him and making his life miserable.

Through all this trouble, though, their sex life stayed the greatest. Meg's psychiatrist used to tell her that she wanted to fuck her troubles away. Maybe he was right, because no matter what else was wrong, when they made love, he still brought her to that sensuous pink cloud, and the earth still moved.

Vince and Meg had always enjoyed spontaneous sex. A certain look would pass between them and they knew. They made love wherever the mood struck them. One night they'd gone out for dinner and drinks at the Wind and Sea in Dana Point. When they left the restaurant, they strolled over to their boat slip. Still no boat, but they had the slip.

Meg started to get amorous and then got downright horny. She traced her finger down the small of his back and pressed her body near to him as they walked, using every seductive lure she had in her bag of tricks. Unable to control his own desires, he took Meg by the hand and, with his key, he unlocked the bathroom door at the marina.

They lunged at each other in hungry need, their mouths seeking each other's and their hands exploring the warm, smooth flesh beneath their clothes. Vince lifted her up onto the counter between two sinks, his hands sliding up the inside of her thighs.

They made steamy love on the counter in the bathroom. In the back of her mind, Meg could feel how cold that damn tile was, but it didn't matter—she was on her pink cloud.

Whatever it was that made Vince stay, whatever made him put up with all the trouble they'd been going through, she was grateful. She loved him, now and forever, through good times and bad, and she knew he loved her, too.

● ● ●

The court appearances and jail visits with Matt, the anxiety and pressure during that problematic time had taken its toll. As much as she loved him and had tried her best to help him, now Meg had lost one of her children for a second time.

Regardless of Vince's unwavering love and support, Meg's depression intensified. Even though she was in bad shape emotionally, she tried to maintain a semblance of normalcy, taking care of her two younger boys, Johnny and Brian, keeping house, trying to keep going from day to day.

On that sunny day in May 1977, though, as she sat down to do the monthly bills, Meg was feeling terribly sorry for herself. While writing out the checks and trying to figure out which bills she could pay and which ones she could stall, she decided to have a drink to ease the tension. Maybe a phenobarbital would make the headache behind her eyes go away and would make this dreary day go by faster. What the hell, why not make it a double bourbon and take a whole handful of pills? Maybe, just maybe, the whole bottle of pills washed down with the rest of the whiskey would take the pain away forever.

Meg began to feel very woozy, and she had a sinking feeling, like she was being pulled down somewhere, somewhere deep and dark. She realized she was starting to pass out. At the very last moment she panicked; she didn't really want to die. Before she passed out, she fumbled for the phone and called the suicide prevention center. She had talked to them on previous occasions when she'd become depressed and had their phone number on a sticker by the phone. Her call was a desperate plea for help.

"H'lo? This is Meg M'reno. I jus' took a buncha pills and I think I'm gonna pass out…" She was so confused she couldn't even remember if she'd been able to give them her address before she lost consciousness.

When the paramedics and police got to the house, there was no response, so they broke the front door in. She was lying in the kitchen on the floor, the phone receiver a few inches from her hand, off the hook. One of the paramedics slipped an oxygen mask over her face, and the other checked her vital signs. She was alive, but just barely. They were loading Meg into the ambulance just as Vinny pulled up.

"Oh, baby," he cried, "not again." He tried to get into the ambulance with her, but the paramedics told him he would have to follow them in his car to the Orange County Hospital emergency room.

Meg stopped breathing and her heart stopped on the way, and the ambulance pulled over to the side of the freeway so the technicians could give her CPR. When she started breathing on her own again, the ambulance continued its desperate race.

In the emergency room, the doctors immediately started an I.V. and pumped her stomach. Meg's throat was sore from the stomach tube for weeks. After her stomach was empty of the overdose of barbiturates and alcohol, next came large doses of liquid charcoal and other medications, both intravenously and orally. Meg stayed in the hospital all day. Later that night she was released to go home for Vince to take care of her. Her whole body was sore, and she was very, very sick.

When she got back from the hospital after this last act of insanity, Vince told Johnny and Brian that Meg had contracted food poisoning and had become violently ill. They didn't need to know of her despair and depression. And except for missing her one son, she resolved from that point on to try to pick up the pieces and create a normal life with Vince and their two other boys. They would enjoy life, take family vacations, do all the things other people did to live a happy, normal life.

Something happened to her in that ambulance that afternoon. Meg faintly remembers after they had performed CPR on her, something or someone spoke to her. Something happened in her heart, and she knew from within her very core of being that NOTHING and NO ONE would ever again drive her to the depths of suicide.

NEVER!!! Something deep in her gut screamed, "I want to live. I don't want to die."

She would never again attempt to take her own life. She felt emotionally changed. From that moment on, she looked at things differently. Nothing and no one was worth giving up the precious gift of life. Nothing was that bad, nothing she couldn't figure out a way to get through. Life was for living, through the good times and the bad.

She thought of the good things and the good times she'd had in her life. The bad times were just setbacks, really. After all, here she was. She had survived the tough times so far. And when she analyzed it, there were far more good times than bad. There were the holidays and birthdays. There were the quiet, intimate moments with Vince. There were the vacations with the kids and the dogs. There were the flowers blooming in her garden. There was her dad who, through the years, had always shown he cared and loved her unconditionally. There was Vince, always there, loving her.

Through everything, she'd maintained a sharp sense of humor, always quick with a wisecrack or a joke. Except during her deepest and darkest depressions, she would see humor in anything, and always had a quick and sincere smile. Her friends often called her Sunny. Maybe humor was a defense mechanism, since she felt so wounded emotionally. Maybe it was her humor and her strong faith in God that had saved her and kept her sane.

Someone once told her that every day above ground is a good day, and that became her philosophy. She would never again attempt to take her life. It was too precious.

13

In the first part of 1979, Meg's father had to go into the hospital to have a hernia operation. Other than his malaria, this was the only time he'd been sick, and he'd never been in the hospital. He was more than a little nervous about it, saying that most of the time when people went into hospitals, they didn't come back out.

Meg and Vince came to the hospital to be with him that morning before his operation. "Don't worry, Dad, we'll be right here. Everything's going to be all right," Meg reassured him just before they wheeled him into the operating room. She knew it would make him feel better and more secure if somebody was there to hold his hand and comfort him than if he had to face it alone.

Irene wouldn't come that morning. "I can't stand hospitals. They make me nervous, and something about the smell makes me nauseous. All those sick people… Besides, it's just a hernia operation. He'll be fine."

Meg and Vince were sitting in the waiting room, doing a jigsaw puzzle, waiting for him to come out from under the anesthesia so they could go in to see him. In the corner, a woman played with her little boy, running a toy car along the armrest of the olive-green plastic chair in which she sat.

The surgery was a pretty standard procedure, but Jim was, after all, sixty-nine years old, and any surgery on a man that age was something to be slightly cautious about. Meg just wanted to be there when he woke up. She knew if she were in his shoes, she'd feel more confident seeing a friendly face when she swam up from the depths of anesthesia. Besides, she'd heard somewhere that patients whose family members were involved in their care and interested in the procedures, before and after, not only did better, but that the staff was more attentive.

"Mrs. Moreno?" Meg and Vince rose to meet the doctor as she walked into the surgical waiting room, still clad in her green gown and operating cap. "I'm Doctor Overby." She reached out to shake Meg's hand.

"Hello, Doctor, I'm Margret Moreno. How did he do? Is he awake yet? We'd like to go in to see him as soon as we can," she said with a smile.

The doctor stood before them. "Do you think we could go over to the couch there and sit down for a moment? There's something we need to discuss."

Vince and Meg walked with her to the green Naugahyde couch in the corner of the room. Thinking the doctor wanted to inform her of her father's postoperative procedures and care, Meg asked, "Does he need any special care after he gets home? I mean, I know he shouldn't be lifting anything or driving for a while. Is there something in particular we need to know?"

They sat down, and the doctor got right to the point.

Putting her hand lightly on Meg's wrist, she said, "There's no easy way to say this. I'm sorry to have to tell you this, but when we got inside, we found that your father's pancreas was cancerous. It wasn't a hernia at all. We removed as much of it as we could, but the malignancy has metastasized, and there isn't much we can do. I'm afraid the prognosis is not very good."

Meg stared at the doctor in disbelief. What was this woman telling her? Her dad couldn't be sick. He couldn't have cancer. Parents were invincible and they would live forever. Her dad would always be there for her to turn to. It was a feeling all children had—that the umbrella of parental care would always be there. Her dad couldn't be sick, couldn't be dying. No, not her dad.

The doctor was saying more words. "… nothing we can do at this point. Because of the advanced stage of the disease, all we can do is send him home to live as best he can for as long as possible. He doesn't have much time. And at some point, all we'll be able to do is try to keep him as comfortable as possible."

Meg was devastated by this news. She turned to Vince with an anguished look on her face. She was overwhelmed with grief, shock and sorrow.

Brushing away a tear, Meg muttered to nobody in particular, "We can't tell him." To the doctor she said, "Please, don't tell him about this. Let him have as much time as possible without this horrible knowledge. What possible difference could it make to his care?"

The doctor thought for a minute, and then said, "All right. We'll treat this as if it were just a hernia operation for now, if you think that's best. At some point, however, he will have to be told the truth."

As soon as she could think of what to say, Meg called her mother at home and told her what the doctor had said. Irene took the news stoically, without much emotion, and no tears.

A few days later Jim was discharged from the hospital

and went home. Doctor Overby acceded to Meg's wishes, letting Jim think he was just recovering from a hernia operation. She warned him not to drive or lift anything heavier than five pounds, and not to start up again with his bowling league for a while, at least until the stitches were out and until he felt up to it. She cautioned him to get plenty of bed rest until the incision healed.

"You're going to feel pretty tired for a few weeks, but after the incision heals, you should begin to feel better," she said.

During the next few months, Meg spent as much time as possible with her dad. Knowing she was going to lose him was heartbreaking to her, and the secret she carried within her heart was a heavy load to bear. She brought her son, Brian, who was now sixteen, over as often as possible. Jim liked Brian, and the two of them spent endless hours together playing checkers and card games, laughing and joking until Jim would tire and have to rest. Sometimes when Jim was very tired, Brian would sit quietly and read to him.

Irene's way of dealing with Jim's illness was to ignore the whole thing. She spent very little time with Jim. It seemed she was always gone, and whenever she was there in the house, she was stoned on prescription drugs and incoherent. During one visit to see her dad, Meg counted three separate times in the space of three hours when Irene took some kind of a pill from her purse, washing it down with a beer.

Jim got weaker by the day, and the pain inside wouldn't go away. He began to question and get angry about why he was feeling so bad.

"Something isn't right, Meg. There's something the doctor isn't telling me. I'm tired all the time, and there's so much pain. It's an effort to even get out of bed. I never wanted to be a burden to your mother or to anybody, but now I need help just to get dressed in the morning." His doctor had been giving him increasingly stronger pain medications, telling him it was medication to reduce the inflammation, but even the powerful pain killers didn't seem to bring him much relief. Sometimes Meg would find him sitting on the edge of his bed, moaning and breathing in short gasps, trying not to cry out and give in to the pain.

After talking to Doctor Overby and the clergy, Meg and Vince, and even Irene, felt Jim should be told the truth about what was wrong with him. Even if he did suspect it, he needed to be told by a loving family member.

"I can't do it. I just can't do it," protested Irene. "I never was very good with sick people."

The responsibility fell to Meg. She agonized over how and when to tell him. Each time she'd go see him he was so sick in bed she just couldn't bring herself to divulge the truth. It took her a long time and many visits to work up the courage to tell him the tragic news.

Finally one afternoon, Meg was sitting and reading to him. He was very despondent over not seeing any improvement. Somehow the opportunity seemed right.

"Dad, when you had your surgery last year, when the doctor got inside, she found more than just problems with your hernia. She found pancreatic cancer. She got most of it, but it had metastasized and she couldn't get it all. There's nothing she can do. We didn't want to tell you about it because sometimes these things go away and get better," she lied. "But at this point, there isn't much more to be done."

She saw tears well up in his eyes, but he didn't say anything about the fact she had just told him he had terminal cancer. He just looked off into the distance for a little while, then hung his head over his clasped hands as he sat on the edge of the bed. He changed the topic of conversation, and for the rest of the time he had left, he never mentioned the word cancer. Before Meg left that day, she bent over to kiss her dad goodbye. As she got close to his face, they looked at each other a long moment, embraced, and both wept openly. No one else was there, and they were both thankful for that. It was a very private moment, a moment of silent caring between two people who loved each other dearly.

Jim became increasingly ill. He was in constant, extreme pain and discomfort twenty-four hours a day. Irene rented a hospital bed and they got a visiting nurse to come in twice a day to help take care of him and administer medication such as morphine through a catheter they'd inserted in his neck, but the pain was so severe that nothing would make it totally disappear.

He couldn't eat, and he lost a lot of weight. Each time Meg went to see him, it broke her heart to see her vibrant, once healthy father, the fun-loving and laughing Jim O'Conner, reduced to a shell of his former self, suffering and riddled with excruciating pain.

On September 29, 1980, they got a call from her mother saying her father had been rushed to the hospital in an extremely serious condition. Meg and Vince immediately hurried to be with him.

As she held his hand by his bedside, Jim kept telling her, "I'm so tired, Meggy. It hurts so much all the time, so much pain. I've got to get some rest or I think I'll go crazy. Oh Lord, honey, I just want to take a nap. All I want to do is get some sleep."

Toward evening he got much worse and he was transferred into the intensive care unit. The doctors told them Jim had only a few hours to live and asked Meg if she wanted him put on life support systems.

"Why are you asking me to make that decision?" she cried. "My mother needs to decide that, not me. I can't be the one to tell you that."

"We've called Mrs. O'Conner, but she seemed unwilling or unable to give us any direction. Mrs. Moreno, we need to know what course of action to take."

Meg didn't want this responsibility. Her mother should be the one to make this decision. But Irene was at home, spaced out on pain killers, and was unwilling or incapable of helping her.

God, what an awful dilemma. Humans are not prepared to take on the role of God, to decide if someone should live or die. Meg prayed for guidance to help her make this crucial determination regarding the father she loved so much. She remembered her dad's last words, telling her how he was in so much pain and stress, and how he was so tired and just wanted to sleep.

Out of all the love in her heart she said, "I don't think my father would want to be put on machines. Please don't take extraordinary measures or put him on life support systems."

She wept as she said it. It was a terrible burden to bear, and a decision she should not have had to make alone.

Later in the evening a nurse came out from Intensive Care and found Meg. "Mrs. Moreno, we think you might like to come in. He's comatose and might not know you're there, but perhaps you would like to be with him now."

Meg's first reaction was that she couldn't do this. Then the nurse very gently explained, "Your father has had as much pain medication as we can give him. We think he's slipping rapidly, but the last sense of a dying person to go is their hearing, and he might recognize that you are near. Sometimes it helps them through the process of dying if they can hear their loved ones around them."

That's all Meg had to hear. Vince and she immediately went into ICU to his bedside. Meg took his hand in hers.

"Hi, Daddy, it's me, Meggy. We're here. Vince is here, too. You're not alone."

They each held his arms and shoulders on either side, rubbing his arms, and they talked and talked about everything, anything, the weather, the kids, how much they loved him, not to be afraid because they were there and loved him, that God was with him.

As they were talking the nurse came over and softly told her, "He's gone." Meg hadn't even known he'd died. He had slipped away peacefully in their arms with the two of them talking to him. Had the nurse not told her, she wouldn't have known he was gone.

Meg ran out of the room and banged her head on the wall in the hallway, releasing all the hurt, pain and tears inside.

That night changed her life. When someone you loved so very much died in your arms, nothing else could get you down that much again. No matter what troubles you went through—being broke or hungry, losing your job, arguments with your husband or children—were inconveniences. That final end, that was the big one. That was what should affect our lives—getting through to the end. Everything else was a learning experience along the way.

• • •

The events of next few days were lost in a mist of mourning. Irene was lost in her own world, so somehow Meg took care of things at the hospital and made the funeral arrangements. She functioned but didn't remember.

Meg asked the funeral home to play "Oh, Danny Boy" at the service. Some people thought it was inappropriate, but she knew he would have loved it. If he could have, she knew her dad would have smiled when he heard his favorite song. She loved her dad very much, and she knew he knew it, all during his life and wherever he was now.

She kept her father's wedding ring and wore it all the time. A day didn't go by that she didn't touch that ring and think of him and love him, knowing he was looking down on her now.

Throughout this whole ordeal—her dad's illness, his hospitalization, his death—her mother was in a chemically-induced stupor. When he died, she certainly didn't react the way you'd expect someone who had been married for that long to someone would have. Irene didn't show any emotion at all. But then again, she was in a daze, a drug-induced euphoria.

A couple of weeks before her father died, Johnny came to Meg and told her the girl he'd been dating was pregnant and that they would be getting married shortly. He loved her and wanted to marry her, and he was sorry to have to tell Meg news like that right then, but since she was pregnant, the wedding would have to be soon. It couldn't have been postponed, Meg guessed, but she was in deep mourning and couldn't think about that right now.

At her father's funeral, Meg was desolate. At thirty-nine, both men in the family who had loved her unconditionally—her father and her grandfather—were gone. Sobbing with grief, she stood by the graveside next to her mother, who stood dry-faced and still as a statue.

Reaching for Irene's hand through her tears, she turned to her mother for comfort, but received none. Irene stood stiffly by the grave at the cemetery and abruptly pulled her hand away. Instead of comfort, Irene turned brusquely and said to her, "I don't know why you're so upset. After all, he was your father in name only."

With a start, Meg stared at her. "What? What did you say? What are you talking about?"

"I mean, he wasn't your real father. Sure, we got married, but he wasn't your father," Irene said cynically. "It could have been one or two others I was with at the time." There were more words, but they washed past Meg's ears like white noise. She stood there immobilized and in shock.

Meg turned her back on her mother, trying to block out the abhorrent words hurled in her face. At first it didn't register, but then the reality of what Irene had said hit her like a slap in the face. The gentle man, the man she had called Daddy all her life, was not her real father?

At home after the services, Meg sat alone in the living room in the dark, trying to piece out the puzzle. Her mother's spiteful words returned to haunt her. Suddenly, she felt like only half a person. She had so many questions. Who *was* her real father? Why hadn't he married her mother? Where was he now? What kind of medical problems did he have that Meg should know about? She felt like pieces of her were missing.

• • •

Vince had always had a clairvoyance about him, and Meg was convinced he had a gift. In desperation, one night a few months later she talked him into getting out their old Ouija board to try to find out any information about her real father.

They lit candles and turned out the lights, and Meg put the board on the kitchen table. Both of them sat, side by side, their fingers lightly touching the pointer. To warm up the board, Vince started off by asking it an easy question. He knew the answer to this one.

"Ouija, does Vince Moreno love Meg O'Conner?"

The pointer, with their fingers poised lightly touching it, moved of its own accord rapidly to the word YES. Vince decided on one more question.

"What is our oldest son's name?"

For a brief moment, the pointer seemed to quiver, then slowly moved to the question mark.

"It knows that Matt's not your son, Vince. He's really only my son by birth. Ask it another one."

"Okay. What is my middle name?" Only a few people knew this, and he'd never even told Meg.

The pointer quivered and began to slide to letters on the board. A-U-G-U-S-T-U-S.

"Augustus? Oh Vince, how regal! It reminds me of a Roman emperor or something."

Now it was Meg's turn to get down to the serious questions. "Oh, Ouija board, do you know who my real father is?" Meg asked.

Almost immediately, the pointer slid across the board to land on YES. Meg was so excited she could scarcely breathe. She had to ask it more questions. She didn't really want to ask the next one, but felt she had to.

"Is James O'Conner my real father?"

Again, the pointer rather rapidly moved to point to a word, but this time it said NO.

"Tell me the name of my real father," she requested.

It took a long time, and the pointer moved very, very slowly. It came to rest on the letter J and stopped.

Meg couldn't figure this out. "What does that mean?" she asked Vince.

"Maybe it can't tell you. Maybe it's an initial or something. Ask it."

"Is the letter J his first initial?" she queried.

The pointer moved to YES.

"What is his last initial?"

Again the pointer slowly moved, and this time stopped on the letter T.

"Ouija, is my father still alive?"

This time the pointer swiftly slid off the board without stopping to point to any letter. Meg was confounded. She decided to ask again. "Is my father still alive?"

Again she got the same reaction.

"I think that means the Ouija is not going to tell us anything more tonight," Vince told her. "We'll try again some other time, baby."

"Well, at least I know his initials now—J.T." She wouldn't give up. She had to find out who her real father was, even if it took the rest of her life. "I'll find him somehow, someday, but he'll never know the kind of love from me that I had and still have for the man who raised me, the man who I'll always regard as my dad." Meg even contacted the television show, "Unsolved Mysteries," to see if they could help her find him, but they decided not to pursue it.

• • •

Eleven days after her father died, on October 10, 1980,

her son John was married. John had asked Vince to be a part
of his wedding's party of best men, and Vince felt very
honored. That day, Vince looked handsome in his gray
tux...the first time he'd worn a tux in his life. John and
Vicky were married in a country club near Mission Viejo.
It was a lovely wedding, but Meg couldn't really enjoy the
festivities. She was still consumed by grief and loss. She
was there physically, but not emotionally.

• • •

Meg kept pushing her mother to tell her who her real
father was. Irene just coldly and angrily spat, "Look, I was
drunk and it could have been any one of two or three guys.
I don't have any idea who your father is. Jim O'Conner had
a crush on me for years, and when I got pregnant he agreed
to marry me and give my bastard child his name. That's all
there is to it. Now don't ever ask me about it again."

The real mystery unfolded when her mother did tell her
that when she was one year old, a knock came at the door,
and when Irene went to see who it was, there was a small
package on the porch. When she unwrapped it, inside was
a little necklace and bracelet addressed to baby Meg. Her
real father knew about her, even though she would never
know who he was.

"Bastard?" Meg shouted at Irene. "I'm not the bastard.
Whoever that guy is, he's the real bastard." Suddenly she
remembered how angry Irene had become when she'd lost
that small piece of jewelry years ago. "Bastard!" she cried
out again. And yet she ached to know who he was.

14

On February 13, 1981, her first grandchild almost died when he was born, but was spared. God does forgive our sins, Meg thought. Perhaps it was karma. Perhaps this was the new little life for her to care for and love.

• • •

Repulsed and appalled by her mother's pill popping, Meg had stopped abusing prescription drugs, but she still liked to party. Even though she loved to drink, Meg considered herself a functioning alcoholic. She took care of business six days a week, not touching even a beer, but on the seventh day, it was PARTY TIME!!

On that special day, she and Vince would go out to dinner and have a few drinks, but then would come home and finish the evening there, playing games, having a few drinks, relaxing in the Jacuzzi, having a few more drinks, playing the guitar and listening to music, having a few more drinks, dancing, drinking, and making love. Meg always finished the bottle. But the difference was, now she partied. No more gloomy blues. She didn't drink because she was depressed or because she wanted to drown herself in a bottle and forget about living. She had no destructive thoughts or self-pity. It was crank up the music, pour the booze, and let's dance!

That summer Meg and Vince had gone out for dinner, had a few drinks, and then decided to go home and change into their Western duds and go to the Crazy Horse Saloon in Santa Ana. They loved to dance and enjoyed country music…in small doses.

They only had a couple of drinks at the Crazy Horse, but were both blind drunk when they left. With the radio blaring full blast, they wove their way home toward Mission Viejo, singing at the top of their lungs.

Their song was interrupted by the wail of a siren. Twisting around in her seat and peering blearily behind them, Meg began to giggle. "Don' loog now, but I thing we've got an eshcort."

Vince glanced into the rearview mirror, and in the space of a few moments, tried to get sober. He pulled carefully to the side of the road and stopped the car.

The crunch of gravel on the road heralded the approach of a police officer next to his door. "Sir, would you please take your license out of your wallet?"

"Hey," Meg said, leaning over to talk out Vince's window, "wassa matter? We weren' doin' nothin' wrong."

"Hush, baby. I'll handle this."

The officer scrutinized the license Vince proffered and then told Vince, "Sir, would you please step out of the car?"

Vince did as he was told, and Meg got out of the car,

too, slamming her door with a resounding thud. The patrolman put Vince through the standard tests to test for drunk driving, and he failed most of them, stabbing his finger into his eye instead of touching his nose, and unable to walk a straight line.

Somehow, Meg found this hilarious and, giggling furiously, she danced along the white line behind him, nearly falling several times.

The officer allowed Vince to return to the car. "Sir, I'm going to have to place you under arrest for driving under the influence."

"What? You're crazy!" Meg protested loudly, arms akimbo. "He's not drunk. Fer cryin' out loud, why doncha guys go arrest somebody's who's committin' a crime! Buncha creeps…person just wants ta go out and have a good time and some jerk hasta spoil everything." Meg was getting louder and more vociferous all the time.

"Ma'am, if you would just return to your vehicle…."

"What for? I din't do anything wrong!" She stood, arms on her hips, hair wild, confronting the policeman.

"I'm afraid, then, that I'm going to have to cite you for obstruction of justice. You'll both have to come along with us. Your husband is in no condition to drive home, or anyplace, for that matter."

The patrolman put them in the back of the police car and drove them to the police station in Santa Ana. Meg was suddenly sober. Vince was led off someplace, and she was put in a holding cell. As the door clanged shut behind her, she felt helpless, terrified and alone.

They were fortunate Vince had plenty of cash with him. After being held for a few hours, he was able to bail them both out. Those few hours in custody were the worst few hours she'd ever spent. Meg felt out of control, afraid of the unknown, wondering what was going to happen to them. The people she saw in the cells frightened her, and she dreaded the thought of being put into a cell with one of them.

When she was finally released, she found Vince in the

hallway on one knee, his arms outstretched, singing, "Mammy." Somehow, Meg failed to see the humor in the situation. Being in jail was no fun, and their little escapade had cost them a bundle. They did most of their drinking at home after that.

• • •

In April 1982 Meg read in the paper that a movie company was auditioning for extras on a movie they were making in San Juan Capistrano, *The Juggler of Notre Dame*, starring Melinda Dillon and Merlin Olson.

"Oh, Vince, let's try out! I've always wanted to be a movie star," she joked. "It's not too far from here, and who knows, we might be hired. It sounds like a ball!"

Vince was all for it. "Hey, yeah, sounds like fun. With my rugged good looks, I could be the next Clark Gable," he joked.

Along with hundreds of others, they were hired as extras on several scenes, working for three days. One night they worked until the wee hours of the morning as the director and producer took and retook the same shot over and over again and again.

Meg had always envisioned actors as living in palatial mansions, driving beautiful cars and living large. She thought making movies was just going onto a set, reading a few lines and then going home early to party all night. During those three days, she and Vince learned that acting was hard work, with a lot of waiting around while the crew reset the lights, cameras, filters and blocking for each and every scene. Sometimes the same scene was redone a dozen times or more.

On the second day, she and Vince were part of a crowd scene being filmed in an old Spanish marketplace, a set created for the movie, at the mission in Capistrano. In this particular scene, the juggler had to toss two balls over his head, and his friend behind him had to catch them. It's pretty hard to hit a target behind your head, and that scene must have required over fifteen takes before it was completed to the director's satisfaction. When he finally yelled, "That's a take!" the whole crew and all the extras broke into spontaneous applause.

The principal players had do some scenes at least a dozen times, and each time they had to give it their all. They had to be "up" and in character, saying their dialogue with convincing freshness. In one scene there was supposed to be an argument, and Meg tried to imagine trying to pretend you were mad at the same person, saying the same lines for a dozen times.

On the third night they worked until two in the morning, in biting cold. The cast and crew huddled around, cupping steaming mugs of hot coffee in their hands in between takes. They were filming a scene where the juggler has his faith restored by the Madonna's statue in a chapel at Christmas.

Watching them work and being involved in the whole process gave Meg a new respect for actors and actresses. They were some of the hardest working people she could think of. It was a business, and they were professionals, trained in their craft and in doing their jobs. In her opinion, they deserved every penny of the salary they made. By the time the three days were over, Meg was exhausted.

When she missed her period that month she didn't think much about it, attributing it to the hard work and stress of working until the early hours in the morning almost all of the three days they were extras in the movie. And in May when she missed it, again she shrugged it off. After all, she was almost forty-one, and it could be the beginning of menopause.

She began to feel sick each day. Thinking it was a touch of the flu, she forgot about it, but it didn't go away. They still partied and drank heavily one night a week, but every time they did, she could feel terrific cramping in her lower abdomen. Her breasts were tender, and she'd put on a little bit of weight. Meg began to suspect she could be pregnant, and finally went to see her doctor.

"Good news, Mrs. Moreno, the rabbit died," he joked as he breezed into the room after she'd gotten dressed. "I'd estimate you're about six weeks pregnant. Now, I know you're over forty, but not by much, and many women your age have successful pregnancies. You'll just have to follow some careful rules."

Meg just sat there and looked at him. She was shocked to find out she was pregnant. She and Vince had given up the idea of having children together years ago. At first she was dismayed by the doctor's news, because she felt she wasn't ready for this. She and Vince had raised her three sons into fine young men, and she was unsure about starting a second family this late in life. And yet, a ray of happiness began to shine in her heart as she thought about finally carrying Vince's child. This would be the only child she and Vince could call their own.

But then the reality of years of hard drinking crashed in on her. Vince and she had been heavy weekly drinkers. What if Vince's sperm had been altered by his drinking? What if her baby had been affected by her alcohol intake? She'd heard of fetal alcohol syndrome and was worried that the baby would be born deformed, or with serious health problems. And then there was the matter of their ages—she was forty-one and Vince was fifty-two.

She didn't know how to ask him this, but she had to. "Doctor…um…I'm worried about whether this baby will be all right. Other than the fact that I'm forty-one, I drink pretty heavily one night a week. I've read something about how alcohol can affect an unborn child."

The doctor thought for a minute, then said, "Well, since you're only six weeks along, most likely if you were to stop drinking at this point there would be no permanent damage. Lots of women have a glass of wine now and then, and then find out they're pregnant. Their babies are born perfectly normal."

Meg shook her head rapidly. "No, no, you don't understand. We're not talking about a glass of wine, or just one drink. I'm talking about some heavy duty drinking, really putting it down. I used to have to drink every night of the week, every day. I think I have it under control now, and I have a system, a routine. For six days I don't touch a drop. But on that seventh day, I *need* to relax. We start out at dinner with a few drinks, and then we party all night. My drink of choice is Wild Turkey, and we usually finish the bottle."

The doctor sat quietly for a few minutes and then asked her, "That's a hundred and one proof, isn't it?"

She nodded affirmatively.

Again he was quiet for a long time. Then he turned to her and said, "I'm not sure what to advise you. There's a strong chance that on the days you drank, you may have caused alcohol-related damage to your unborn child. On the other hand, the baby could be born quite normal. There's just no way to tell. Given your age and these particular circumstances, if you wanted to choose an abortion, I would endorse the procedure. I'm not recommending it, mind you, I'm just saying I wouldn't be opposed to it if that were your decision."

An abortion?! Her Catholic upbringing shrieked at her that it was wrong. She wanted this baby, the only baby that she and Vince would ever have, yet she was afraid. If it were deformed or retarded, she wasn't sure she could cope with it. She had enough problems coping with life on a day to day basis as it was.

When she left the office, Meg got in her car and just drove and drove and drove. How ironic, she thought, steering the car automatically without really seeing. Drinking would probably be the reason she would have to have an abortion, but God, how she wanted a drink right now. She pulled over to the side of the road and tried to remember when her drinking had started to become so heavy. She couldn't remember. She guessed it had built up gradually over the years. You didn't just wake up one Tuesday morning and decide that this was the day that you'd start abusing alcohol.

She knew that her suicide attempts had been screams for help, and figured her abuse of alcohol was a way to block out all the pain that she still embraced in her heart and mind.

Her mind flashed back to the holidays. My God, how many of those had she ruined for the entire family? She could be a real pain in the ass. Often she got hysterical, especially after Matt left home, yelling and cussing her family out over trivial things. Oh yeah, it was a pretty sight. And now, here she was, sitting on the side of the road, facing the reality of the price for all those drunken rampages. Her hands held the front of her belly tightly as she leaned her forehead against the steering wheel and sobbed.

She finally composed herself and pulled back onto the road. On the way home, she stopped at the Big Bear market and bought two sirloin steaks, potatoes and makings for a Caesar salad. As she set the table and made dinner, she searched her soul for answers. After dinner, as she and Vince were sitting in the glider on the patio in the fading evening light, she told him.

"Vinny, I'm pregnant," she blurted out.

He turned to face her. His face registered first surprise, then delight, and he reached out and pulled her to him in a bone-crushing hug. "Oh, baby, that's great! Oh, man! When did you find out?"

"Well, you know how I've been feeling sick lately? I've missed two periods, but thought maybe I was just starting to go through menopause. I went to the doctor today, though, and he said I'm six weeks pregnant."

"Six weeks! Well, well, little Mama," he joked and patted her flat stomach. "Now we'll hear the thunder of tiny feet around here again." He'd always wanted children of their own, and the only other time she'd gotten pregnant with his child, she had miscarried.

"There's just one problem," she went on, removing his hand from her stomach and trying not to burst into tears. "Sometimes when a woman is my age, there can be complications. One of the most common is that the child is born with Down's syndrome."

The smile on his face faded into an expression of sober concern. "There's more, isn't there? I can tell by your voice."

"Yes, there *is* more," she replied in a quavering tone. "The doctor says there might be a chance that the baby has been affected by the nights when we party. The alcohol...the fact that on that one night we drink so much..." She had to stop and take a gulp of her iced tea before she could go on. "He says the baby might be deformed, or even severely retarded. There's no way to know for sure."

Vince was quiet. He stared vacantly out at the colorful flowers she'd planted. His eyes were sad as he looked back at Meg. This was killing him, but he knew how devastated she must feel. She'd wanted to have a baby with him ever since they'd met. His arms went around her shoulders in silent empathy.

"We have to decide whether or not this baby should be born, Vince. As much as I want this child, I don't know if I'm capable of taking care of a baby that might be handicapped. The doctor said if we wanted to get an abortion, he'd endorse our decision. But it's a sin. It's murder. Oh, I'm just so confused right now." And with that, she began to cry, quietly at first, and then with deep, anguished sobs.

Vince and Meg spent almost every waking moment of the following two weeks weighing their choices and agonizing over a decision. They met with the doctor again to learn more about what the consequences could be. Many hours were spent in church, praying for guidance to make the right decision.

After a lot of advice, a lot of soul searching and a river of shared tears, she and Vince decided to abort their baby. Her doctor made the arrangements, and the date was set for the second of June.

When she woke up that morning it seemed unusually cold, especially for June. She went into the bathroom and brushed her teeth, deliberately avoiding her reflection in the mirror. She slipped out of her short nightie and got into the shower. The hot water created billowing clouds of steam, and still she felt frigidly cold. As she rinsed the soap from her body, her right hand gently touched her stomach, and suddenly she was overcome by tormented sobs. She was glad Vince was already downstairs, out of earshot.

She dried herself quickly, still feeling icy cold. At least she wouldn't have to look at herself in the mirror to put on any make-up because they had told her not to wear any, not even nail polish. She always felt she looked awful without her usual liberal application of cosmetics, but today she didn't care. She would look as ugly on the outside as she felt on the inside.

She put on her underwear and a pair of slacks and a pullover sweater, then went downstairs and told Vince she was ready. They quietly embraced, then put on their sunglasses and walked out to the garage. When Vince started the car, the radio immediately sprang to life, playing the oldies but goodies that she always loved listening to. Vince looked over at her and his hand reached down to silence the music.

It was foggy as they pulled onto the freeway. Even with the warm sweater on, she was still shivering with cold. The clinic was about twenty minutes from their house—the longest twenty minutes she ever spent in a car in her life.

Vince tried to talk a little on the way there, not expecting any answers, just talking. "Don't worry, honey, everything will be all right. You know, even with no make-up, you're still beautiful." His tenderness pierced her wall of pain, and she smiled at him. He returned her smile with a wink and a tight squeeze of her hand.

When they arrived at the clinic, there were batches of forms to be filled out, and then they had to talk with a counselor, who tried to get her to stop crying.

"After all, we're only going to remove a small piece of tissue," she said efficiently.

A small piece of tissue? Meg didn't believe that for a minute. This was her baby that she was terminating. This was not some lifeless, inanimate blob of tissue, like a wart. It was a life, her unborn child.

After they performed some tests, Meg changed into a short hospital gown and was instructed to sit in the small, stark waiting room with some other patients. As she sat there with hot tears streaming down her face, she was appalled at the conversations she overheard, along with giggling and laughter. One young woman, a pretty blonde, leaned over and said to her, "Come on, don't worry. There's nothing to it. I've had it done several times." Even though she hadn't had anything to eat or drink since early the evening before, Meg thought she was going to throw up. For her, this was a tragedy.

Far too soon they called her name and led her into the surgery room. They helped her up on the table, placing an I.V. tube into her arm, and her feet in the stirrups. Never had a room seemed so bright and white, a table so cold and hard. Tears ran out of the corners of her eyes and into her ears. Her last blurry thought as she went under the anesthetic was to run, run, RUN!

When she came to after the procedure, she was still crying. Had she been crying all the while, even under anesthesia? She didn't know. Only when she had suffered a miscarriage many years ago had she ever felt so hollow, empty and dead inside.

Vince's face was grief-stricken when he came to take her from the recovery room, but she couldn't find anything to say to comfort him. She was too consumed with her own pain and sense of loss. She was so groggy she didn't remember much of the ride home. It didn't matter how long it took, because at that moment nothing mattered, and she didn't know if anything ever would again.

At home, Vince settled her on the couch in the family

room so she could rest. Even though he didn't want to leave her, he had to go to work. Thankfully, the anesthesia made her groggy enough so that she slept on and off most of the afternoon. In her periods of wakefulness she tried to watch television, but it seemed like every other commercial she saw was for baby food and diapers, reminding her of what she had lost.

That evening, Vince came in with flowers and a bottle of Estee Lauder perfume. He wasn't bringing her gifts like he usually did for an occasion of celebration, but as an act of love in a moment of shared tragedy. He leaned over the couch to give them to her, and they fell from his hands as he gathered her in his strong arms, his tears and hers mingling as they wept together over their loss.

Meg cried for days, filled with a feeling of unbearable emptiness. The guilt and remorse over what she had done was overwhelming.

Logically, Meg knew that their decision was probably the only thing they could have done, and was medically sound. Still, she couldn't justify the fact that she'd committed murder.

An abortion isn't over with the day you have it done. You live with it in your heart for the rest of your life, and you pray that God will forgive you and that He will understand why you had to do it.

• • •

Both Vince and Meg were raised Catholics, but when they had married in 1964, they'd been married outside the Church, with a minister performing the rites. For their nineteenth wedding anniversary in 1983, they both strongly wanted to have their marriage consecrated in their faith. For the marriage to be recognized and blessed according to the doctrines of the Catholic Church, they would have to attend classes and counseling sessions, complete tons of paperwork, and go to confession.

Meg dreaded the idea. She would have to confess to the priest what she had done.

That day she stood at the door of the church for a long time, trying to gather up her courage. Holding her rosary, she genuflected and made the sign of the cross, then walked down the aisle and turned toward the confessional booth. She felt like she was hyperventilating, so stopped to take two or three deep breaths before she stepped inside.

She knelt before the patterned cane screen and addressed the priest behind it. "Bless me, Father, for I have sinned." The moment she uttered these words through the screen that separated her and Father Connely, she began to tremble from head to foot, her stomach twisting in anxiety and dread. No more words would come out of her mouth, and she felt like throwing open the small wooden door of the confessional and running as fast and as far as she could. But she knew she couldn't, not if she and Vince were to have their marriage blessed by the Catholic Church. It was something that they both had wanted for a very long time.

At times theirs had been a stormy marriage, but it had always been a strong union, each of them devoted to each other through thick and thin. At that moment, however, Meg had very serious doubts about whether she was going to be able to complete this confession. Her knees felt glued to the padded kneeling bench, and she had no choice but to go on.

They had gone through an enormous amount of red tape just to get this far. Each had to search for their baptismal records, hers from Illinois and Vince's from Los Angeles. All that was finally completed, and now came the hard part. They each had to make a thorough confession, something neither of them had done in many years. They both regretted that they had strayed so far from their Catholic upbringing, but even more than that, she was clutched with terror at what she now had to confess.

"And how, my daughter, have you sinned?"

When she was finally able to speak, she said simply, "I

have had an abortion." She'd never spoken those words aloud to anyone.

There was a roar of silence from the other side of the confessional that lasted a long, long time. Meg's palms began to sweat and she felt a headache coming on.

When the priest finally did speak, the first thing he said to her was, "Do you realize that you have committed murder?"

With tears in her eyes, Meg admitted and accepted her sin and was ready to do penance to expiate her transgressions. Her penance was very severe and went on for weeks. But whatever penance the priest could give her, no matter how long it went on, she knew it wasn't enough. How could sacrifices and prayers atone for the taking of a life?

Meg was very thankful she had Vince to share the decision with her. He didn't just say that the decision was up to her. They had talked it over, prayed together, cried together, and they had made the agonizing decision together. He was there with her to share in the whole ordeal and afterward, too. Her heart was grateful for his love and support.

Each year after that she had an indelible reminder of their tragic decision. Each Christmas season, whenever *The Juggler of Notre Dame* appeared on television, Meg could pick herself out in the crowd scene and would remember that when the movie was made she was pregnant, carrying Vince's child.

She'd always wonder if maybe she'd been carrying the little girl she never had, since she had three boys and always wanted a girl so badly. How sad for Vince that he had raised her three children and they never got to share a child of their own.

She was glad that her sons had finally picked up the pieces of their lives, and were no longer involved in drugs. Matt had been through a stint in the Navy and had settled in Hawaii, with a good job working at the Outrigger Hotel on Oahu. Johnny had graduated from high school, gotten married, and was working for the Orange County Fire Department. Brian was still trying to find himself, traveling with his girlfriend, but at least he was no longer following a destructive path.

She and Vince were alone. Romance had begun to blossom again for them, and the shared terrible experience of the abortion had brought them even closer.

Even through all the times when their marriage had been sorely tested, Meg felt that when they took those marriage vows, they didn't say, "Do you take this person for better and better?" They had said, "Do you take this person for better and for worse?"

It disheartened her sometimes to see young people, and people of all ages, give up on each other. If only they would remember the promise they made to each other as they were first married. That promise was for better and for worse, in sickness and in health, not just for the good times, the happy times. That's what marriage was all about. You pledged your love to someone through thick and thin. You had to take the bad with the good.

15

Meg flopped down on the stairs and wiped the sweat from her brow. She'd spent the entire morning cleaning the house from top to bottom. It didn't take nearly as long as it used to, now that the boys were grown and gone. In a way, she sort of missed picking up the trails of socks, books, and sports equipment that they always left behind. It was visual proof that her home was full of life. But lately she was beginning to think this was too much house for just her and Vince. For crying out loud, it still took at least five hours to get her cleaning done, if she wanted to do everything in one day, and this wasn't how she envisioned spending her free time after the kids left home.

"My God," she mused out loud. "The kids really are all

gone, and here I sit in this big, empty house." The last ten years, the years they'd spent in this house, the years the kids were growing up, started to play like a movie through Meg's mind…the bad times, the drunken times, the good times. Suddenly Meg felt very sad, thinking back on how tough it had been trying to be the one in the middle all the time between Vince and the kids.

If she were honest with herself, she'd have to admit that one of her biggest mistakes during those years was wanting so much for the boys to love Vince as much as she did. She'd tried so hard to undo the harm that all of her mother's brainwashing had done to them. When Vince would make mistakes with the boys or be unfair, Meg would take the blame for Vince's boners, and maybe in the kids' eyes that made her the bad guy. She wished she'd been more honest in the relationship and let the chips fall where they may. If Vince looked like an asshole because of the way he handled something, so be it. But no, there she was, always trying to make him look good. She guessed the boys probably saw through it all, anyway, but she sure would have handled things differently if she had the chance to do it all over again.

Meg took a deep breath and got back to her cleaning. She made up her mind to talk to Vince that night about putting all this behind them and looking for a smaller house someplace else. Maybe they could make a fresh start, just the two of them.

That night she approached Vince with her idea. "Boy, I'm pooped! I must have spent five hours cleaning this house today. Vince, what do you think about moving to a smaller place? I know this house will sell and make a pretty good profit, and if we get something smaller maybe we could get a place with a little land, maybe get a horse." Her voice was pleading. It was probably every little girl's dream to have a horse, and Meg's mother would never even let her have any kind of pet.

"Yeah, they've been building up a lot east of here, and

I'm sure I could get some landscaping contracts in that area," Vince said. "There's no reason for us to rattle around in this big old house, just the two of us. Let's go look for some property this weekend and see what we can find."

• • •

It took them nearly six months of looking, but finally they found a beautiful ranch in Sun City on five acres of land. "Oh, Vince, I absolutely love it," Meg had gushed when she first saw it. "It's just what I imagined our ranch would look like." The house was low, surrounded by eucalyptus trees, with a natural rock fireplace in the rustic pine-paneled living room.

Vince especially liked the rugged open beam ceilings and the flagstone walkway from the gravel drive. He stood outside the house and looked around at the open space and took in a deep breath of fresh air. He envisioned the possibilities in this place, and how they could make the home beautiful with flowers and shrubs. It would be a good place for them, a place for Meg to have a horse, a dog or two, something to care for. He knew she missed having her boys at home.

Their Mission Viejo house sold for a good price, and in late 1983 the two of them became urban cowboys. The house was small, just 1400 square feet, but it was comfortable for the two of them, and the ranch already had fences and buildings that would be perfect for housing the animals.

Meg went to the small local library and checked out books, spending hours reading and learning everything she could about horses and farming. She and Vince would pore over books at night and attend horse auctions on the weekends, not bidding, just watching the people who sold and bought the animals. Several dogs and cats became members of the family.

Finally, they felt they were ready to buy a horse. They

weren't planning to breed or race, just wanted a horse for riding and pleasure use. Meg told Vince, "If we can, I'd like to get a quarterhorse, you know, a horse like the cowboys ride. They're supposed to be really smart and very gentle."

They were looking for a horse two or three years old, maybe one that had been raced and let out to pasture, either a mare or a gelding. At the auction, they saw several animals they liked, but none that Meg felt an affinity for. Maybe it was silly, but she felt like she'd know the moment she saw it when they found the horse that was right for them. Suddenly, Meg excitedly pointed to a beautiful thoroughbred with a dark brown mane and tail.

"Vince, that's the one. Oh, isn't she a beauty?" They looked her up on their program and discovered she was three years old and the starting price was right. Not to put all their eggs in one basket, they picked out two or three others they were interested in, too.

In her heart, Meg had already named the horse Spirit, because the horse's markings reminded her of the ghostly haze that hung over the California land in the early mornings before the warm sun burned the mist away. She felt a kinship to this animal and prayed they would be able to acquire her.

The auction progressed, and soon Spirit was up for sale. The bidding was moderate, but the price got a little higher than they wanted to go.

"Six hundred," called a man from the right-hand side of the barn.

"I have six hundred, six hundred, will anyone make it six-fifty?" intoned the auctioneer.

Vince saw the hunger in Meg's eyes and decided they could spend a little more than they'd budgeted. "Six-fifty," he said, raising his hand.

"I have six-fifty, six-fifty, is there a bid for seven hundred?" There was silence except for the pawing of hooves and occasional whinny, and the creak of the metal chairs.

"Sold for six-fifty to the gentleman in the blue shirt."

Meg realized she'd been holding her breath and let it out with a sigh. She leaned over and gave Vince a squeeze. It was more than they'd planned to spend, and she loved Vince more than ever that moment for splurging on that horse.

The next week was spent hunting for an affordable used horse trailer and buying tack and feed and other necessary supplies for the new member of their family. They brought Spirit home that next weekend to their ranch, the Circle B.

Getting her into the trailer was trickier than they'd anticipated. Spirit was absolutely positive she didn't want to get in that thing. Vince was at her head, trying to lead her in, while Meg manned the gate, ready to close the door. As Spirit passed Meg, standing on the ramp, her hoof came down hard on Meg's tennis-shoe-clad foot. The horse stood there, back legs tensed, straining at the reins in Vince's hands.

"Vince! Get her off! She's on my foot!"

Vince backed the horse up and tied her to a handle on the trailer so they could examine Meg's foot. Her shoe was cut and her foot hurt a lot. "I don't think we better take off your shoe until we get to the doctor's, baby. It could be broken and it would swell. We'll never get your shoe back on."

Meg agreed and hopped over to sit in the car. Somehow Vince managed to get their horse into the trailer alone and they headed for home. Getting Spirit out of the trailer and into the barn was a much easier task, and when Vince had her settled, he rushed back to the car to take Meg to the doctor.

Sure enough, several small bones in her foot were broken, and she had to stay off of it for a few weeks, sitting with it elevated on a pillow in the house. Meg fumed, furious at herself. She should have known to get riding boots right from the start just in case something like this happened. Now she wouldn't even get to ride her splendid horse until her foot was healed.

Before long Meg and Vince had three horses and a beautiful champagne-colored burro named Shaney. Unlike the horses, who possessed dignified personalities, Shaney was a clown, always into something, chewing on the pine trees, stealing Vince's tools, or trying to hug and push Meg too tightly against the side of the corral.

Meg was exhilarated by the love and trust her horses gave back to her. There was no greater thrill than seeing her young green colt named Poco completely relax and trust her the first time she showed him a saddle. At first he trembled from his hooves to his ears, and his eyes were as big as plates as he considered the alien thing Meg held in her hands. But she talked softly to him and let him sniff and even bite the saddle, and soon he was ready to do whatever she was going to ask of him.

When Vince's two-year-old horse named Sunny developed colic and lay down in the middle of the corral kicking at his belly, Meg sat in the corral with him with his head in her lap and calmed him until the vet arrived. With all the members of her menagerie, Meg ruled with a calm and loving hand. She had a natural rapport with and love for animals, and they returned that love to her.

Being an inexperienced horsewoman, in the course of getting to know these thousand-pound animals and how they acted, Meg was bitten, chewed, stepped on, kicked, run away with, and attacked by horses, but it was an experience she wouldn't trade for anything in the world. Her enthusiasm for life and love for all living things made a game of it.

• • •

They soon discovered, however, that the move to Sun City was not a good one. Although the area had been growing and there was a lot of new construction, it was proving difficult for Vince to rebuild his landscaping business in the desert. There was a whole new set of rules to learn, new types of plants, a new clientele to develop.

One evening Vince sat at the little desk in the living room, shuffling papers around, making piles and moving bills from one pile to another, trying to juggle the figures. Meg noticed him hard at work and brought him an ice cold beer and started rubbing his shoulders.

"Is there anything wrong, hon? Anything I can do to help?"

Vince sighed and turned to look at her. He didn't like to bother her with finances. Usually, he was able to make things work out, but for months now things had been going from bad to worse. Practically every proposal and bid he'd made had been turned down. Their money had almost run out, even their savings from the sale of their Mission Viejo home.

"Baby, I hate to say this, but we're going under. I'm not getting any new jobs, and some of my old customers have quit. We might have to sell off the animals pretty soon, and we're going to have to do something drastic just to keep this place. There's no way we can pay all of our bills this month, and there's even some here from two or three months ago that I just can't find the money for."

Meg was stunned. She knew Vince's landscaping business had slowed down, but she had no idea the situation was so critical. They lived a pretty frugal lifestyle— didn't go out much, didn't spend a lot on clothes. They spent most of their time on the ranch.

She stood in silence with her hands on his shoulders for a while as his words sunk in. Well, they'd just have to make the best of what life dealt them. Somehow they'd get through this. Looking down at his worried face, she told him, "It's okay. We'll get by. Maybe I can get a job someplace to help out. At least we'll have money for food and the rent."

Meg used to be a make-up artist, so after trying to find work in vain, she even applied at the local mortuary to see if she could get a job applying make-up on the bodies. If she would have gotten that job, she would have been grateful to get it. Desperate people do desperate things.

The money was going out faster than it was coming in. Suddenly they were behind on all their bills and were being harassed constantly by creditors and bill collectors. They called at all hours until the phone had to be disconnected. Finally, they couldn't make the house payment.

They took a second mortgage out on their house to meet their bills, and now they had a double payment to make. At times they were so hungry they would fill up on peanut butter and bread or hot dogs.

"Vince, I think we ought to go down and apply for food stamps. Our income probably qualifies us for some kind of help, and at least we'd eat better than we have been." She was humbled and ashamed to have to resort to this, but they were desperate. They were losing everything they'd worked for over the past twenty years—the house, the horses, their cars, everything.

It looked absurd to be driving over to the welfare office in their Lincoln Continental to apply for food stamps, but they were hungry. They were turned down for food stamps and public assistance because Meg's dad had willed her a tiny piece of land by Salton Sea, so they didn't qualify. Too bad they couldn't have eaten sand, Meg said to herself.

Meg looked again through the want ads, trying to find a job to help out. For several months she worked in Hemet as a salesgirl at a department store, but her bad back caused her such excruciating pain from being on her feet all day, she was forced to quit. She would get off work and then just sit in her car and cry from the physical pain.

Next she was a receptionist and helper in a pediatrician's office in Hemet. She answered phones, filed, and greeted patients. She liked the job, and it was much easier on her back than standing all day behind a counter. The doctor saw primarily MediCal patients, and many of them were referrals from agencies regarding child abuse cases. Meg couldn't stand seeing the children who were victims of parental abuse. It was beyond her understanding how any adult, especially a child's own parent, could hurt someone so young and innocent. Sometimes when she'd see the evidence of a beating, she'd get so sick and angry she'd have to leave the room. It was emotionally exhausting, and Vince finally told her that it just wasn't worth it. He urged her to find something else, a job that wouldn't rake her over the coals each and every day.

It was an emotional, depressing time for them. When there's a financial disaster, there's no one else to blame, so you blame each other. They got into terrible arguments that nearly destroyed their marriage.

One night in a fury, Vince lashed out at her. "That goddamn zoo out there eats better than we do. If we got rid of all those freakin' animals, we might be able to make it!" Instantly, he regretted his words. In his heart, he knew how much her animals meant to her. They were like her children, now that her sons were grown and gone. But he was getting desperate.

She was past the point of tears herself, and angrily retorted, "Yeah? Those animals only eat about a hundred twenty dollars worth of feed a month. I can't get rid of my animals. It would be like selling my children, and you know that. And hey, don't try to put all the blame on me. If you could get a few jobs, then we wouldn't be in this mess!"

They both said words they didn't mean that night, and some nights the tension was so great between them, Vince ended up sleeping on the couch in the living room. They blamed each other for their problems, and at one time or another, each thought about how much easier life would be alone.

When trouble comes, sometimes it rends people apart, but to Meg their marriage vows were made for the lean days, too. Marriage wasn't just for the good times, the rich times. It was for always, through thick and thin. One night after another of their biting arguments, she knew she had to do something to end this bitterness. She came up to Vince from behind and wrapped her arms around his waist.

"Oh, Vinny, this isn't getting us anywhere. Fighting won't solve our money problems, and blaming things on each other won't do anything but tear us apart. And it looks like we're all we've got right now."

He turned and gently cupped her face in his strong hands. "You're right, babe. Even if we lose everything, I don't want to lose you."

At last they figured out they could either go through the court appearances and the bankruptcy together or alone. They chose to maintain a united front and weather the storm together.

● ● ●

In early 1985 she saw an ad in the paper for a receptionist in a beauty salon. She'd had years of experience in make-up, and they had owned and run their own beauty shop, the Satin Doll in Downey. This job was right up her alley. Vince had managed to land a couple of good landscaping contracts, and if she could get this job, they just might be able to keep their ranch.

When Meg applied at Canyon Lake Hair Productions, she was scared to death. She was no spring chicken compared to the other girls she saw in the shop, but she needed this job desperately. The owner was a woman about her age, and Meg recognized humor and the light of laughter in her eyes from the moment she saw her. Something in the woman compelled her to tell the truth about what was happening in her life right then.

When the owner, whose name was June, asked her about her experience and why she thought she should get the job, Meg looked her right in the eye and replied, "First of all, I know everything there is to know about running a beauty shop, from top to bottom. We had our own salon, the Satin Doll, in Downey for several years. Secondly, I'm old enough to have been around for a while. I'm not gonna get up and get married and get pregnant and disappear after a year or two. Finally, I desperately need this job. We need money to eat, to keep our horses, and so we might be able to keep them from foreclosing on our ranch."

"Well, that was a mouthful," June said. "But I like your honesty. I've been looking for someone who would stay with us for a while. We've had three receptionists in the last six months, and it takes time and money to train them. I think you'll stay, and I can use your experience. The job is yours if you want it."

It didn't pay much, but it helped pay the bills. The women she worked with were funny and gave her emotional support while she and Vince were going through the foreclosure of their home. It might have been the only thing that kept her sane.

Despite all their efforts, they were evicted and desperately needed to find a place to live. They had ten animals—two horses, one burro, two dogs, and five cats they loved with all their hearts. They had to find a place to live where they could take their extended family with them.

They had to move into a house that was right next door to the ranch they had just lost. At least there was room for the zoo, as Vince called it. From the back door of the house, she would look out at the ranch she had loved, the view and the peacefulness, and cry.

The night they moved in, Meg kept all of their cats inside so they would get used to the new place. There was an uneasy aura about it, an uncomfortable feeling that maybe this was not a happy place. That night the cats howled, prowled and cried all night long. Meg spent a sleepless night, too, interrupted by strange dreams and strange sounds.

They had signed a lease for a year, and Meg was soon to wish they hadn't.

The next day Meg put on work clothes and began what

seemed to be the insurmountable task of cleaning up the place to make it livable. The previous tenants apparently had an aversion to soap and water and must not have owned a vacuum cleaner. When she opened the dish cupboard to clean and line the shelves, she found piles of debris piled in the corner.

Taking her rag, she muttered, "Boy, whoever lived here before must have been lousy housekeepers." She swept the pile into the paper bag she was holding, then noticed what it consisted of. Peering into the bag, she saw packages of used and unused syringes, hash pipes, and other drug paraphernalia.

The next cupboards she opened were empty, but inside the doors were painted pentagrams, upside down crosses, and other signs of Satanism. Meg slammed the door closed and quickly crossed herself. She hurried outside with heart beating fast and sank into a lawn chair. No wonder the cats were uneasy and she couldn't sleep at night. Something evil had been left in this house…something disturbing and wrong.

They spent the rest of the first week sanding, painting and disinfecting everything, trying to remove all traces of the hideous markings. Removing the filth and covering the evil signs with paint helped the appearance, but the longer they lived in that house, the more they could feel that something was not right.

The first time Meg tried to use the washing machine, the whole kitchen flooded. She'd been out in the garden and Vince was in the barn with the horses, and they'd both returned to find water washing from the utility room into the kitchen and slowly seeping out to the carpet in the living room.

"Vince, quick, get some towels!" They hurriedly formed a dam to the living room and tried to mop up the soapy water before it caused too much more damage. Vince called a plumber to remedy the problem.

"Mrs. Moreno, here's your problem. The drains are

clogged with pieces of cut straws and paper. And there's some kind of clear plastic envelopes down there, too. How long have you people lived here, anyway?"

"Just a little over a week. What in the world would all that stuff be doing in the drains?" Meg asked.

The plumber looked at her and then confided, "There used to be a bunch of young kids that lived out here. They pretty much kept to themselves, but folks in town said they used to be into drugs pretty heavy, and had some pretty wild parties. Sheriff finally got a conviction on two of them, and then they all cleared out. That stuff is probably from using cocaine."

The carpet did get wet, and the smell was intolerable. "God, Vince, this place stinks! It smells like urine, human urine!" Meg had the carpets professionally cleaned at least three times, but it didn't seem to help. They ended up ripping out the carpets and resanding and refinishing the hardwood floors underneath just to get rid of the smell.

The first time they tried to use the fireplace in the living room, the entire house filled with smoke, even though they opened the flue. After it cooled down, Vince investigated.

"Meg, I found the problem," he called, with his head inside the chimney. "There's a bunch of trash stuffed up the chimney. Get me the hoe and a drop cloth, and I'll try to pull it down out of here." He pulled and scraped, and from inside the chimney came wads of old rags. Wrapped in one bundle was the desiccated carcass of what looked like a dog. Ashen-faced, Vince solemnly wrapped up the hideous remains and disposed of it, then bravely attacked cleaning the chimney of other accumulated filth and dirt so they could use the fireplace.

Everywhere they turned, there were more repulsive surprises. Meg's animals were jittery and tense, as if they sensed the house and land were haunted by evil spirits.

But they'd signed a lease and had to make the best of it. Meg bought scraps and remnants of wallpaper cheaply and tried to fix up the place to make it homey and livable.

They cleaned and scrubbed inside and out, and Vince planted flowers and shrubs to alleviate the barren landscape.

Meg continued to work during the day at the beauty salon as a receptionist. Many days she was emotionally upset when she went to work. Sometimes she'd get so sad she'd have to go in the ladies' room and cry and then come back to the desk. She hated going back to that house. They spent a lot of time window shopping, riding around, anything not to have to go back to that horrid house.

Christmas of 1986 marked six months in the devil house. There was no money for presents, but Meg roasted a chicken and did the best she could to have a festive Christmas dinner. They did their utmost to keep it a blessed event and count their blessings, such as they were.

The true test of people is not how well they function during the good times, but how well they function and live their lives during the worst of times. They were surely going through a period of trial, but if they could just stick it out together, somehow things had to get better. Meg felt tough times don't last—tough people do.

• • •

During their last few months in the devil house, Vince was able to land a couple of very big projects that promised very good pay and a steady income. It turned their lives around again. It never ceased to amaze Meg how humans never knew from one day to the next what lay around the corner.

Upon the advice of an attorney, they managed to break the lease. Now they were paying rent from month to month, all the while hunting for something else. In the beauty salon where she worked, one day Meg was chatting with a realtor and mentioned they were looking for a house to lease, someplace with room for their animals.

"Right now we're living in this horrible house that used

to belong to some satanic cult or something. It's just hideous. I don't think I've slept a solid night for six months, and I know my animals can tell there are evil spirits there. We're looking for something else, someplace with room for a couple of horses and a burro and a few dogs and cats."

The realtor handed her a business card. "You know, there's a home in Canyon Lake on five acres of land you would like that might be available. It's on a hill with a magnificent view of the lake and the hills, and is customized beautifully inside. It's been for sale for quite some time, but hasn't sold, so the owner might be willing to take a lease."

Meg's first thought was they wouldn't be able to afford it, so she put the woman's card in her purse and didn't think about it too much. She and Vince kept looking for another place to live. Now that the lease was no longer effective, she didn't want to stay in the devil house a day longer than she had to.

After they'd looked around a while and didn't find anything, she remembered the card in her purse and called the owner, who agreed to show them the house. It wouldn't hurt to look, she reasoned.

As they drove up the long, curved driveway to the house, Meg's breath was taken away. The house itself was covered with rock and blended in with its natural surroundings. Inside was even more stunning. Meg rushed from room to room, her eyes alight with excitement. It was exquisite! There was a rock spa in the master bedroom, and it had a twenty-two-foot bar in one separate room just for entertaining, with a view of the mountains and Canyon Lake.

Meg took Vince aside. "Oh, Vince, it's just perfect! I guess we shouldn't get our hopes up, but it would be a dream come true if we could live here." When they started talking to the owner and he told them what he wanted for the lease, she gasped. They'd been paying $900 a month for the devil house, and he only wanted $1000 a month. It took everything she had to control her excitement. Their prayers had been answered, and she knew they had truly been blessed.

In June 1986 they moved into this beautiful 3400-square-foot mansion on the top of a hill overlooking Canyon Lake. That night the cats walked around as if they owned the place and were happy as larks. They slept curled in tight little furry balls on the king-sized bed or nestled into the curve of Meg's back. Wrapped in Vince's arms, she knew their life was getting better.

In Canyon Lake, Vince's landscaping business began to grow, and Meg began writing. With her love for life and her new-found joy in every day on earth, she knew she had stories and adventures inside her to share with the world. She wanted to write children's stories and books. There was something innocent inside her, something untouched and pure, that had never been sullied, no matter what trials and problems in her life she'd been through.

Both felt as if they'd been tested—their love, their sense of humor, their will to live. But they hung in there and fought like hell and survived. Meg figured whatever cards you got, you played them. And she felt it was even kind of exciting to contemplate what the next hand would be that the Dealer had in store.

16

Meg usually arose before six in the morning, always having loved the quiet early morning hours of each new day. She'd put on a pot of coffee and then go feed her cats and dogs. Bundled in her green chenille robe, she'd go outside to fill the numerous bird feeders that she'd placed strategically around the house so she could watch the colorful masters of flight and song. When she awoke this morning, however, it was pouring down rain and there was a bone-chilling wind blowing. At the kitchen table, she poured a second cup of coffee and decided that since it was only twelve days until Saint Patrick's Day, this would be a good time to stay indoors and hang up all of the fun decorations.

Meg enjoyed decorating this beautiful house for every

holiday. She usually went overboard, and then it would sometimes take days to get everything down and put away. She loved the decorations and didn't want the holiday to end. One year, her Christmas decorations were up until nearly the middle of January.

She was rummaging in the closet in the spare room for the box of decorations when the phone rang. Putting the box down by the kitchen door, she answered the phone, surprised to hear the voice of her Aunt Ellie from Hesperia.

"Meg," Ellie said with urgency in her voice, "something is terribly wrong at your mom's house. She called me and I could barely understand her, but I was able to make out that she'd fallen during the night and had been laying there for a long time. I told her to call 911 and that I'd call you."

Meg's heart lurched and she felt a sense of alarm. "Okay, Aunt Ellie, I'll try to call her or go over there. I'll call you back as soon as I know something."

Meg tried to call Irene, but there was no answer. At least the phone wasn't off the hook. She frantically started calling the hospitals that Irene usually went to. At Doctor's Hospital in Lakewood they confirmed that Irene was there.

Meg shook Vince awake. "My mom's had some sort of fall or accident, and is in Doctor's Hospital. I don't know what's wrong, but we have to get there right away! Hurry and get dressed!"

She quickly ran a comb through her honey-blonde hair. No time for make-up. She'd wear her sunglasses. It would take well over an hour to get there, and she was frantic with worry. Before they left, she hastily called her aunt back, and then they left.

The 91 Freeway seemed to be more crowded with early morning traffic than ever, and the rain made the going slow. Meg was a nervous wreck all the way to the hospital.

When they got there, they hurried to see Irene first, then asked to see her doctor, because she seemed to be in a great deal of pain. Meg was even more alarmed by how confused

Irene seemed. She couldn't even tell her what had happened.

When the doctor finally came to talk to Meg and Vince, he told them, "Apparently your mother lost her balance in her living room and fell between a chair and table. She lay there for several hours, drifting in and out of consciousness. We feel she has badly bruised one of her kidneys, and that's what is causing her so much discomfort. We have her under observation, and she's on antibiotics at present."

Meg and Vince stayed with Irene for a while, but then had to drive back to Canyon Lake so Vince could go to work. Before they left, Meg told her, "You just rest and get better. We'll be back on Thursday to see you, Mom." Irene didn't seem to hear her.

Meg called the hospital twice on Wednesday. The nurse who answered the phone said Irene was resting, but there wasn't much change in her condition.

On Thursday, Meg was more concerned than ever. Irene seemed to be in even more pain than before, and now she was acting delirious. She'd ramble on and on and cry and say things like, "Boy, wait till Jim finds out about this. He's really gonna raise hell."

"Vince, this is crazy. Dad's been dead for ten years. What in the world is she talking about? Something's not right. I'm going to have the nurse call the doctor."

When the doctor came into the lounge where they were waiting, he explained that Irene's kidneys had been damaged more than they'd first realized, and that now they were actually shutting down, causing toxins to build up in her system. "That's what is causing her delirium. We have to get those poisons out of her. Unless we're authorized to start dialysis, your mother will continue to deteriorate and the prognosis is not favorable."

What was he saying? Was her mother going to die? With trembling hands Meg took the paper that the doctor was holding out to her and signed it. It broke her heart to see Irene like this, and she prayed that the dialysis would help. Vince put his arms around Meg and she cried softly.

On days when Meg was unable to get to the hospital, she'd call two or three times a day to see how Irene was doing. The nurses said they felt she was showing some improvement.

When Meg and Vince went back, they were both filled with new hope. Irene looked and sounded much better. She was alert and was no longer talking gibberish. She was even cracking jokes with her doctor when he came into the room to see her. Aunt Ellie and her husband and some of Irene's friends came to see her that day, too.

While they were visiting, a nurse came in. "I'm sorry, folks, but this little lady needs to go down for her dialysis treatment now. It takes at least an hour, so you might want to come back later. There's a coffee shop in the basement."

Meg patted Irene's hand and said, "See ya tomorrow, okay?" She and Vince followed Ellie out and then stood in the hall visiting with Ellie and Irene's friends.

Vince was anxious to get back to work. "I should be heading back home, hon. That rain's coming down pretty good again. Why don't you wait for me in the downstairs lobby, and I'll pull the car around?"

Meg lit a cigarette while she waited for him. She was extremely relieved that Irene seemed so much better. As she waited, in a corner of her mind, she heard the hospital speaker making announcements. "Doctor Edelman, report to surgery, Doctor Edelman." And "Doctor Grant, please come to the pharmacy, Doctor Grant." Then "Code Blue in dialysis, STAT."

Her blood ran cold. Could it be Irene? She stubbed out her cigarette and ran up to the receptionist. "My name's Meg Moreno. My mom's just gone down for dialysis. I heard the Code Blue on the speaker. Can you please find out for me if there's anything wrong? Please hurry! My mom is Irene O'Conner."

The woman said she'd try to find out and picked up a phone. In a few minutes, she put down the receiver and said, "I'm sorry, but your mother has had a heart attack. They're working with her right now."

Meg gasped for air and ran blindly to the front door to tell Vince to park the car again. "It's Mom! She's had a heart attack!"

Sitting in the waiting area, each minute was an eternity. Every time they asked, they couldn't get any information. Meg was going crazy. What was going on? How was she? Meg paced and smoked and prayed. And prayed. "Please don't let Irene die. Please God, please."

After what seemed like an infinity of time, the lady at the desk called Meg over and said they had Irene stabilized. She was being transferred to a room in the Cardiac Care Unit and Meg could go up and see her in about twenty minutes. Thank God! Irene was still alive!

When they approached the room, Meg didn't know what to expect. She'd mentally tried to prepare herself for anything, for the worst, but her heart took a leap of joy when they came in and found Irene propped up in a sitting position, alert and talking to them. Meg and Vince stayed with her as long as the nurses would let them. Meg fed Irene little ice chips from a small cup and tried to reassure her that everything was going to be all right now. All too soon, the nurses told Meg and Vince they would have to leave but they could come back early the next day. They assured them that Irene was stable now and would probably rest comfortably through the night. Meg kissed Irene and told her they'd be back early in the morning.

The two of them got home about ten-thirty that night, exhausted and hungry. They fixed some scrambled eggs and toast before wearily dragging themselves into bed. Meg was too wound up to sleep right away, so she said her rosary and lay close to Vince, trying to relax enough so she could catch a couple of hours of sleep.

About an hour and a half after they'd gotten to sleep, the phone jangled them awake. Vince groggily fumbled for the receiver. He listened in silence, then handed the phone to Meg. It was the hospital calling. Irene had suffered a massive heart attack and a stroke. They needed Meg to come back to the hospital immediately. Vince was already putting his clothes on, and Meg quickly did the same. During the long, rainy drive to Lakewood few words were spoken. Meg's mind was racing, and she scarcely heard Vince the few times that he did mutter anything.

Even in her worst imaginings, Meg could never have been prepared for what she saw when they walked into Irene's room. Her mother was on a ventilator, and there were tubes coming out of her body everywhere. Her head was turned to the side and her eyes were closed stiffly. There was absolutely no response at all when Meg tried to talk to her.

When Meg first saw her mom she'd started to collapse, but regained her legs and knew she had to do whatever it took to get through to Irene. She had to let her know she was there, then she would wake up. Meg just knew she would. She had to! Meg needed to tell her how much she loved her. They hadn't always seen eye-to-eye, and Irene hadn't always been the perfect mom, but no matter what, Meg loved her.

"Mamma, it's me, Meg. Mamma? Mamma? I'm here, Mamma. Vince is here, too." Meg's voice got louder and louder, but it was no use. There was nothing, absolutely nothing. Nothing but the damned machine with its constant wheezing and beeping.

Meg felt as if she were going mad. She slumped into a chair next to her mother's bed and kept talking to her. Any time now she would hear her and respond. She just knew she would. It would just take a while. Meg and Vince kept stroking Irene's arms and watching for any small sign of recognition.

Irene now had four different doctors taking care of her. Meg and Vince requested to see all of them separately so they could get independent evaluations of Irene's condition. Each of the doctors said the same thing. There was no hope. Irene had suffered a massive heart attack and stroke and now had irreversible brain damage from which she could never recover. Her kidneys had stopped functioning and she was only being kept alive by the machines. The reality was that there was no hope of her ever coming out of the coma or ever improving. The doctors suggested that Meg sign a no code order stating that no further heroic measures be taken to keep Irene alive.

Meg had to back up against a wall to support her weak legs. How could this be happening again? she thought. First her dad, and now Irene. How could she do what they were asking of her? How could she make that final decision?

She sank feebly into a chair and sat with her hand on her forehead, shading her eyes. Vince put his arm around her and said softly, "It's a tough decision, but one that only you can make."

Meg smoked and paced nervously, then she and Vince talked and cried some more. She called Irene's minister and asked him to come to the hospital. Aunt Ellie and Uncle Robert were still there, so she asked their advice. When the minister arrived, they all spent a great deal of time with him, exploring any and all options. There seemed to be no use in prolonging her life when she would never return to being the person she once was. Yet, it was a decision Meg didn't feel comfortable making. These kinds of resolutions should only be made by God, not humans.

At last the horrendous determination was made. Meg signed the damnable document with quaking hands and eyes blurred with tears. Suddenly she felt detached from the entire unreal situation, as if she weren't even there. If she couldn't separate herself from this incredible pain, she was sure she would lose her mind.

Eighteen hours after signing the no code order, Irene died.

Blessed numbness took over now, and Meg functioned like a robot, calling the people she had to call and doing the things she had to do. She called Matt in Hawaii and Johnny in Murietta.

She was unable to get ahold of Brian because he was on the road, driving from New York with his lovely fiancee and all their belongings. At last he was moving back to California. Meg had missed him terribly during the years he'd been gone.

She gave instructions to the rest of the family that when Brian called each day while he was on the road, he was not to be told. She would tell him when he got here. She got a lot of resistance from the rest of the family, but she was adamant. The weather was awful on the road, and Brian had enough to think about. She was in the middle of one tragedy and didn't need another one. She took full responsibility for her decision and prayed that Brian would understand and forgive her.

After Meg made all the calls that she had to, she went to her typewriter and typed a letter to Irene. She would ask the minister to read it at the funeral. She knew she'd never get through reading it herself. Meg needed to put her thoughts and feelings of the moment on paper so she could read it any time she wanted to.

"Mamma, we weren't always as kind to each other as we should have been, and I guess you could say we've had a pretty stormy relationship. But through it all, I've always loved you with all my heart. I just wish you could have known that. I know you loved me, too, in the best way that you could. I deeply regret any pain that I have caused you. It seems your life was filled with more pain than any one person should have to bear, both physical and emotional pain. My prayer, from the bottom of my heart, is that now you are held gently and securely in our dear Lord's arms and you will forever know joy and the eternal love in His heart. I hope He can tell you how much I truly did love you. Goodbye, Mamma. I'll see you again someday. Your daughter, Meg."

• • •

Matt arrived the next day from Hawaii, and he and Meg and Vince went to Irene's apartment in Bellflower to pick up what they needed to take to the funeral home at Rose Hills in Whittier.

On the way there, Matt told Meg, "A few months ago I got a strange letter from Grandma Irene. She said that if anything happened to her, I was to look for a very important document and a letter that she had hidden in her bedroom."

Meg was puzzled by this cloak and dagger business. After all, Irene didn't own anything of value and had no money in the bank. It was probably just some personal request that Irene wanted fulfilled.

It took them a long time, but they finally found the envelope Irene had described. Matt took out the papers and started reading the letter aloud. All of a sudden his voice trailed off. In a stricken look, he glanced up at Meg and Vince and said, "I don't think I want to read the rest of this."

"Go ahead," Vince said. "What could it be? Just read it."

Matt held out a letter from an attorney. "Grandma has disowned you, Mom."

Meg felt as if someone had just slowly run a very dull, long knife through her heart. There must be some mistake. She grabbed the document from Matt. There it was in black and white, all very legal. Irene had publicly and legally disowned her.

Meg's eyes flashed back and forth between Vince and Matt. She forced out a long breath of air and then cupped her hand over her mouth to hold back the screams of pain. This just couldn't be true. All she'd ever wanted was for Irene to love her, and now her mother had legally said for all the world to know that she hated the very day that Meg was born. A flood of overwhelming suffering filled every fiber of Meg's body. No words would come out of her mouth. She just kept looking around the living room that she had been in so many times before, shaking her head and occasionally touching her hand to her trembling lips.

After several minutes, Meg straightened her back and, in a soft voice, asked Matt to come into the bedroom so they could pick out some jewelry and clothing for Irene to be buried in. Meg knew she would have to get through the next couple of days before she could even begin to understand or comprehend what her mother had just done to her. Besides disowning her, Irene had appointed Matt as her executor, and had requested that he handle her funeral arrangements and take care of all her possessions. Apparently she hadn't wanted Meg to touch, let alone have, any of her belongings.

Matt was staying with Vince and Meg in Canyon Lake, and that night when they got home the weather turned even more fierce than it had been all week. There was blinding rain, and the wind was blowing so hard it blew some of the shake shingles off the roof. The howling of the wind matched the howling agony in her heart. God must be angry. Was He angry at Irene for what she had done, or was He angry at Meg for not being the perfect daughter? Meg guessed that they'd both failed each other.

Meg asked Matt if he would deliver the eulogy at Irene's funeral, and they sat down at the kitchen table to compose the words for him to read. After she'd written it out, Meg made a strong request. "Matt, please stick to the eulogy. Don't bring up past history and open up old and very painful wounds." She was referring specifically to the three and a half years that Matt and his brothers had spent with Irene after Meg's divorce. As hurtful as those years had been to Meg, oddly enough they seemed to be a badge of honor to Matt. It wounded her to the quick. Matt agreed to his mother's request, and they began to get things ready for the next day, a day during which Meg knew she'd need every crumb of courage that she could dredge up from the very core of her being.

Vince watched Meg as she got out her black skirt and black linen jacket to wear the next morning. If only there were some way he could take some of the pain from her and put it on his own strong shoulders.

On the morning of the funeral Matt said he needed to stop and get some smokes. The trip from Hawaii had been very expensive for Matt, and Vince had been supplying him with cigarettes, beer, and little things like that. Matt also said he wanted to stop by a flower shop near Rose Hills to pick up some fresh flowers. He refused any financial help for the flowers. When they got to the mortuary, Matt trimmed all the stems off the flowers, then lovingly and carefully strung each flower head onto heavy thread to fashion them into a beautiful lei. He then took the lei into the viewing room and placed it around his grandmother's neck. Meg was deeply touched by this loving farewell and was very proud of her son.

At the chapel, midway through the funeral service, the minister read the letter Meg had written to Irene. When he got to the part that said, "Through it all, I have always loved you," Meg leaned forward with her hands to her face and sobbed loudly and uncontrollably—wretched sobs that tore through her body. Vince, crying too, kept his arm around Meg's quaking shoulders.

Matt walked to the podium next and started to read the eulogy. He paused, then put the prepared paper to one side and started extolling how wonderful it was that his grandmother had taken him and his brothers in and had cared for them. Until that moment, Meg had never seen any reason to tell her sons what had really taken place, how Chuck and Irene had cruelly torn them from her loving arms and heart. At that moment she deeply regretted that decision to shield them from the ugly truth. The anguish of losing her mother, being disowned by her, and now being submitted to this cruelty from Matt was more than she could deal with. She felt as if she had been cast into a searing, living hell.

But there was even more to come. At the end of the

service the minister said that the family could have a few moments of private viewing before they closed the casket. Matt rose and came to Meg and said, "Come on, Mom. You and I and John will go first."

A dazed Meg looked incredulously at Matt and said, "What about Vince? He's family."

Matt replied, "No, Mom, he's not blood family."

Meg couldn't believe her ears. She bit the side of her lower lip and then said firmly, "Fine. You and John go say goodbye to your grandmother. I'll say my goodbyes with my husband." She reached for Vince's arm and strongly and steadily held on for dear life. She'd seen the wounded look in Vince's eyes, and she hugged him tightly. They stayed at Irene's side for several minutes, just the two of them.

In the car during the procession to the gravesite, Meg looked at Vince and then turned to Matt and said, "Don't either one of you say a word to me." She wasn't trying to shut Vince out, but at this moment she needed to be left completely alone.

After the funeral the whole family went to Meg's cousin's house, where Meg slowly started to relax and her emotions began to subside.

Meg made a serious mistake that night. On the way back home, she convinced Vince to stop in Lake Elsinore and pick up some liquor. "We've been through a horrible day, and maybe it'll help us unwind."

Once again Meg's weakness for alcohol would cloud her judgment. Everything was fine for a while. Matt, Vince and Meg relaxed, talking and comforting one another. But then all the pain of the day flooded back over Meg and she started in on Matt.

"Why did you think it was necessary to bring up the very things I asked you not to? You know it hurts to hear about how Irene took you boys away from me."

"I just wanted to thank her for taking care of us. It was a wonderful thing for her to do. Especially since you couldn't take care of us."

"Who told you that? Her? I never wanted to give you boys up, but Chuck and Irene conspired together to steal you away from me because Irene didn't like Vince. I know she's spent years poisoning your mind against Vince, and it isn't fair."

Between the booze and the still boiling emotions, Meg and Matt got into a very heated argument, to the point where Matt came close to striking his mother.

Vince had been very quiet up to that point, figuring it was better to let the two of them work out their problems. But when Matt nearly struck Meg, Vince jumped in and ended the whole ugly scene by throwing Matt out of the house. That was it! He'd had enough. Vince had always been Meg's biggest defender, and now, when she was most vulnerable, he had no choice. He hated what Matt had put Meg through that day and didn't know if he could ever forgive him.

• • •

In the days after the funeral Matt and Johnny sold or disposed of all Irene's possessions. Brian was still on the road from New York, so he didn't even have a chance to express any requests that he might have had regarding Irene or any keepsakes from her.

For weeks after her mother was buried, Meg couldn't sleep. When she did finally doze off, she'd have horrifying nightmares. With her nerves frayed to the point of collapse, she fell to her knees one day in front of her crucifix and cried out, "Help me. I can't go on like this. I can't do this by myself. Please, God, help me!"

That night she slept soundly, with no bad dreams to frighten or terrify her. From that day, she never forgot to thank her Redeemer for hearing and answering her desperate plea.

Meg still carries the letter that she wrote to Irene in her purse, but it doesn't break her heart as badly when she reads it now.

In the weeks that followed, Meg found an outlet in writing, and has written some wonderful music and poetry. She'd walked through a little bit of hell again, but it wasn't going to beat her. There was too much to be thankful for each and every day, and she never wanted to lose track of that. Not for Irene. Not for Matt. Not for *anyone*.

17

Meg stood back and surveyed the effect. She was feeling pretty pleased with herself right about now. She wasn't much of a seamstress, but couldn't find exactly what she wanted for curtains in her kitchen, so decided to try to sew some herself. It had taken a while to figure out the pattern, but now she had beautiful lace curtains in her sunny yellow kitchen.

Ever since they'd moved into their new place, Meg's personality had undergone a subtle change. Always one to look for the bright side, she was even now more positive and cheerful, greeting each day with expectation and joy. Vince and some of her friends had started calling her Sunny, saying that the sun seemed to find a place to rest in her happy eyes.

Glancing out the kitchen window she noticed the bird feeders were nearly empty, and went to refill them. She kept several for the many colorful birds in the area, and loved their graceful flight and melodious songs. The world was so much richer for her with animals and birds around.

Coming back inside, she decided to play her keyboard for a while before she sat down to write. She'd been working on some poems and a children's book lately, putting some of her own experiences with her sons into story form. Sitting at the keyboard in the rumpus room overlooking the golf course, she started to play.

Suddenly her concentration was rudely interrupted by jabbering bluebirds from the feeders. It wasn't just their usual loud shrills; these cries had a real edge of panic. With the melody of "Satin Doll" lost to her, she went to the window to see what was causing all the commotion. When she saw what all the birds were screaming about, she felt the blood drain from her head and the hair bristle on the back of her neck.

There it was, all four-and-a-half feet and fifteen rattles of serious business. Meg's hands gripped the sides of the sink and her knees began to shake. As the birds screeched, she saw Henry, her goofy German shepherd, curiously watching the moving snake. Henry was so stupid he'd probably try to play with the dang thing. She knew she had to do something, and fast!

She went to the gun cabinet and took out the .22 rifle, straightened her back and her resolve, and went outside. She walked around the house, planning to approach her target from the rear, and called, "Henry…Henry, come here!" The dog loped around the corner with a big sloppy grin on his face, and Meg quickly put him inside.

The snake was only about twelve feet from the back door. She raised the rifle and took careful aim. Just as she was about to squeeze the trigger, she lowered the gun. She realized she'd be shooting into decorative rock and that there was a propane tank just off to the left. She rapidly